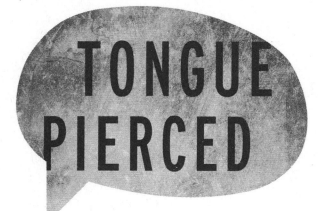

TONGUE
PIERCED

# TONGUE PIERCED

### how the
## WORDS YOU SPEAK
### transform the
## LIFE YOU LIVE

# NELSON SEARCY
### and
## JENNIFER DYKES HENSON

David C Cook®
*transforming lives together*

TONGUE PIERCED
Published by David C Cook
4050 Lee Vance View
Colorado Springs, CO 80918 U.S.A.

David C Cook Distribution Canada
55 Woodslee Avenue, Paris, Ontario, Canada N3L 3E5

David C Cook U.K., Kingsway Communications
Eastbourne, East Sussex BN23 6NT, England

The graphic circle C logo is a registered trademark of David C Cook.

LCCN 2014948632
ISBN 978-1-4347-0874-8
eISBN 978-0-7814-1285-8

The Team: Alex Field, Tim Peterson, Amy Konyndyk,
Nick Lee, Helen Macdonald, Karen Athen
Cover Design: FaceOut Studio, Emily Weigel

Printed in the United States of America
First Edition 2015

1 2 3 4 5 6 7 8 9 10

102914

*To my family, who modeled for
me the power of words.*

—Nelson Searcy

# CONTENTS

# ACKNOWLEDGMENTS

**Nelson Searcy:** My ongoing journey toward a tongue-pierced lifestyle has been a rocky one. It all started in 1989 when I become a follower of Jesus. My life and my tongue were both transformed by the power of the gospel. Since that time, many godly men and women have taught me about the power of words and have held me accountable to a higher standard for my language. These folks include, but are not limited to, my parents (Alton and Patsy Searcy); pastors I worked with early on (Bobby Gantt, Ralph Carpenter, Boyce Gregory, and Rick Warren); and some dear friends, mentors, and accountability partners in my life (Milton Hollifield, Jimmy Britt, Michael Jordan, Scott Whitaker, and Kerrick Thomas).

For major contributions to this book, especially for chapters 6 and 9, I must thank my fellow Journey pastor and previous coauthor, Kerrick Thomas. Kerrick and I have written and preached hundreds of sermons together. He consistently makes what I do stronger. I just wish I had more stories from fifth grade (inside joke!).

I must also express a huge thanks to the members of The Journey Church, in all of its locations, for their ongoing support and prayers. The teachings in this book were first written in community with, and presented live before them. I love doing church with each and every one!

I also want to offer my sincere appreciation to the team at Church Leader Insights. They have helped make this book—and especially all of its accompanying resources—happen. They have no idea of the impact their faithfulness is having on people around the world. Thank you to Scott Whitaker, Sandra Olivieri, Kimberly Pankey, and the entire kingdom-minded team!

Jennifer Dykes Henson has been a partner and cocreator on my last twelve books. To my ongoing amazement, she continues to reach new levels with each book. More so than even our previous books, this one has her life and fingerprints all over it. Quite frankly, this book would not have happened without her. Her skills as a writer, editor, and interpreter are hard to overstate. During this project, she not only served as my coauthor and helped birth the book you hold, but she also birthed her first baby—a beautiful little girl. The book turned out pretty good, but the little girl is amazing. Brian and Jennifer are great parents and great members at The Journey Church.

It has been a pleasure to work on this first project with the team at David C Cook. Working with Alex Field once again has been a delight. Alex was the editor for my very first book many years ago and has been a true champion ever since. Thank you to Alex and the entire David C Cook team!

Finally, I must thank the love of my life, Kelley, and my young son, Alexander. Kelley and I celebrated twenty years of marriage while I was completing this book; Alexander turned eight. For a guy who writes about the power of words, I'm often too reserved in expressing my love for them both. Kelley, I love you now more than ever! Alexander, yes, I will come tuck you in before you go to sleep. Love you, little man!

**Jennifer Dykes Henson:** I have been passionate about understanding and harnessing the power of words for many years. Being able to pour that passion into this book has been a true labor of love.

Thanks to each of my family members and friends whose stories became part of these pages. One of the greatest pieces of writing advice out there is to write what you know. What I know about the power words have to shape lives comes largely from studying how that power has affected the people I love most. To all who find strands of their lives included here, thank you for giving me the leeway to use what I know to illustrate larger truths.

My partnership with Nelson Searcy through the years, and especially on this book, has been nothing short of incredible. I am continually humbled and excited to be involved in the magnificent work God is doing through him. Nelson, thank you for inviting me to the office for that first meeting almost ten years ago and for all the ways you've encouraged our partnership to grow and evolve since. Each year—and each book—is more fun than the last!

Thanks to my husband, Brian, for being a constant source of love and support. Now that we are parents to a precious baby girl, that love and support has taken on new levels of meaning. Brian, thank you for filling our lives with laughter—and for building towers with Isabelle while I go into my writing closet each day. I love you!

Finally, thanks to God for once again giving me the opportunity to engage in meaningful work that will, hopefully and prayerfully, influence the lives of those who find it in their hands for the better.

*Chapter 1*

# THE POWER OF WORDS

*Words have an inherent power, a force capable of lighting one's paths and horizons. Used correctly and positively, words are the first building blocks for success and inner peace. Used incorrectly and negatively, they are capable of undermining even the best of intentions.*

Stephen R. Covey

*Death and life are in the power of the tongue.*

King Solomon (Prov. 18:21 NKJV)

*Once upon a time …* Countless stories throughout human history have begun with these four words. They have introduced tales of joy, tragedy, victory, defeat, love, and sacrifice to us for centuries. As children, hearing these four words let us know that something significant, something fantastic was about to follow. We listened, and the once-upon-a-time stories we heard shaped our worlds. As adults, we may not hear these words often, but every story we encounter begins with them, whether spoken or implied—including your story and mine.

Even though they likely weren't said aloud in the delivery room on the day you were born, your story began with a definite sense of *once upon a time.* As you made your entrance, a new tale opened: Once upon a time, a woman gave birth to a baby. That baby grew, learned, and matured. Now a full-grown individual, that person holds in his or her hands a book on the significance of words that could greatly influence the direction of his or her story from this point forward. But I'm getting ahead of myself. For just a moment, let's look more closely at the significance of *once upon a time.*

A group of sociologists intrigued by the impact words have on daily life recently conducted a study on the most powerful words in the English language.[1] They took an interesting approach. Instead of looking at individual words, they set out to discern the most powerful four-word phrase, the most powerful three-word phrase, the most powerful two-word phrase, and the single most powerful word in our collective vocabulary. You've probably already figured out what they found the most powerful four-word phrase to be: *Once upon a time.*

This phrase resonates with us deeply because we all live in a story. Every day, the story of your life and mine is being played out on the stages we've created for ourselves. These stages are full of interesting characters, conflicts, and plot twists. Who we are, what we do, who we love, our fears, passions, dreams, and goals— all of these things merge together to create our own stories, just as surely as the details and plot lines of the great fairy tales and classics that actually begin with *once upon a time* come together to tell those. Each of our lives is its own unique tale. And each one hinges, whether we realize it or not, on the elemental building blocks that comprise every story ever told—words.

No story gets very far without the collection of words that brings it to life and directs its course. So it is with our own. The words we use have a monumental effect not only on the immediate details of everyday living but also on the overarching trajectory of the story our lives are telling. Our words have the potential to open doors of opportunity for us or to close and seal them shut; they can nourish and build up our relationships or tear down the people we love. The words we speak to ourselves—our self-talk, if you will—have the power to shape our subconscious view of our worth and our abilities, thereby determining the actions we take (or don't take) on a daily basis. And the words we say to and hear from God are critical to the story we live both on this earth and when our time here is over. In short, our words create our lives.

Speaking of God, it's no surprise that *once upon a time* registers with us so profoundly. The phrase is a direct derivative of the opening line of the most important story ever told—God's story, the story in which each of our lives is a subplot. Genesis begins,

> In the beginning God created the heavens and the earth. The earth was formless and empty, and darkness covered the deep waters. And the Spirit of God was hovering over the surface of the waters.
>
> Then God said, "Let there be light," and there was light. (Gen. 1:1–3)

In the beginning, God said, "Let there be," and there was. Out of nothingness, he spoke our world into existence. Genesis continues,

And God saw that the light was good. Then he separated the light from the darkness. God called the light "day" and the darkness "night."

And evening passed and morning came, marking the first day.

*Then God said,* *"Let there be* a space between the waters, to separate the waters of the heavens from the waters of the earth." *And that is what happened.* God made this space to separate the waters of the earth from the waters of the heavens. God called the space "sky."

And evening passed and morning came, marking the second day.

*Then God said,* "Let the waters beneath the sky flow together into one place, so dry ground may appear." *And that is what happened.* God called the dry ground "land" and the waters "seas." And God saw that it was good. *Then God said,* "Let the land sprout with vegetation—every sort of seed-bearing plant, and trees that grow seed-bearing fruit. These seeds will then produce the kinds of plants and trees from which they came." *And that is what happened.* The land produced vegetation—all sorts of seed-bearing plants, and trees with seed-bearing fruit. Their seeds produced plants and trees of the same kind. And God saw that it was good.

And evening passed and morning came, marking the third day.

*Then God said,* "Let lights appear in the sky to separate the day from the night. Let them be signs to mark the seasons, days, and years. Let these lights in the sky shine down on the earth." *And that is what happened.* God made two great lights—the larger one to govern the day, and the smaller one to govern the night. He also made the stars. God set these lights in the sky to light the earth, to govern the day and night, and to separate the light from the darkness. And God saw that it was good.

And evening passed and morning came, marking the fourth day.

*Then God said,* "Let the waters swarm with fish and other life. Let the skies be filled with birds of every kind." So God created great sea creatures and every living thing that scurries and swarms in the water, and every sort of bird—each producing offspring of the same kind. And God saw that it was good. Then God blessed them, saying, "Be fruitful and

multiply. Let the fish fill the seas, and let the birds
multiply on the earth."

And evening passed and morning came, marking
the fifth day.

*Then God said,* "Let the earth produce every sort
of animal, each producing offspring of the same
kind—livestock, small animals that scurry along
the ground, and wild animals." *And that is what
happened.* God made all sorts of wild animals,
livestock, and small animals, each able to produce
offspring of the same kind. And God saw that it
was good. *Then God said,* "Let us make human
beings in our image, to be like us. They will reign
over the fish in the sea, the birds in the sky, the
livestock, all the wild animals on the earth, and the
small animals that scurry along the ground."

> *So God created human beings in his own image.*
> In the image of God he created them;
> male and female he created them. (Gen.
> 1:4–27)

God didn't simply think through what the oceans and continents should look like and then they appeared. He didn't draw a
blueprint and gather a team to get things started. He didn't write
out a description of the sky and the stars and the fish and the birds

and then breathe those things into being. No, his words alone set the world in motion. From the beginning of time, words—God's words—have been the tools that carry the power to create reality. And he has passed those tools to us, filled just as surely with the power to create and shape our lives. In fact, you and I are never more like God than when we use our words to speak the truth of his will for our lives into existence.

## THE POWER OF LIFE AND DEATH

Oh, but how easy it is to forget the inherent power of our words. We gloss over their significance because they are commonplace to us. We take them for granted the way fish take water for granted. We are used to talk; it just is. We are full of, surrounded by, and constantly inundated with words, words, words. Stepping back and seeing the weight and impact of our ingrained linguistic choices takes intentionality. But when we are able to do just that, we will begin to see that each of our little, carelessly thrown around words actually carries the power of life and death. Don't take it from me; King Solomon, widely considered the wisest man to ever live, said so himself: "The tongue can bring death or life" (Prov. 18:21).

Life-and-death issues are nothing to take lightly. Until we start realizing that our word choices carry enormous consequences, we will continue to underestimate how they work for us or against us.

What you say today will—not *can*, but *will*—do one of two things: either lead you down a path toward a more purposeful, abundant life or move you toward destruction. Not physical destruction necessarily—though words can definitely be a catalyst for health issues—but the destruction of relationships, careers, momentum, joy, peace, hope, and contentment. In his essay "War of Words," Paul David Tripp wrote:

> We think that words are not that important because we think of words as little utilitarian tools for making our life easier and more efficient, when they are actually a powerful gift given by a communicating God for his divine purpose....
>
> You have never spoken a neutral word in your life. Your words have direction to them. If your words are moving in the *life* direction, they will be words of encouragement, hope, love, peace, unity, instruction, wisdom, and correction. But if your words are moving in a *death* direction, they will be words of anger, malice, slander, jealousy, gossip, division, contempt, racism, violence, judgment, and condemnation.[2]

As you and I become more conscious of the way we use language, we can begin to take advantage of its power to create the lives we want. In the process we can stop inadvertently sabotaging others and ourselves with words that bring death and destruction. If knowledge really is power, then intentional awareness is the live wire.

Still, we should be let off the hook just a little. Our ignorance on this issue isn't completely our fault. Our understanding and manipulation of language is largely a learned behavior. Most of our harmful speech patterns are etched into our subconscious from an early age. Have you ever opened your mouth to speak to your children and heard your mother come out? Have you ever said something to your spouse only to be struck by how much your comment sounded like your father? Maybe you've found yourself in a conversation with a coworker or a friend and heard a tone escape from your lips that you hate—but one that's been pointed in your direction many times in your own life.

Those innate patterns reflect our early experiences with words; they are the result of conditioning that began before we even knew how to speak. Before you ever said "Ma-ma" or "Da-da," you began to internalize the meaning and tonality of the conversations taking place around you. When you started finding your voice, you learned to talk by repeating what you heard your parents and other family members say. The words of our closest relatives literally become our words, until we develop words of our own. Even when we begin to craft our language in the ways we want, those initial subconscious linguistic roots hold strong. Without awareness and intentionality, we are destined to repeat the patterns we grew up with—which can be either a blessing or a curse.

Did you like the way your parents spoke to you when you were a child? If not, hopefully you have been intentional about making changes in your own word choices when addressing your children. The way you speak to them now is likely the way they will speak to their own children twenty or thirty years from now. Your words will influence not only your own life's direction but also the lives of generations after you. Similarly, think about how your father spoke to your mother, and vice versa, while you were growing up.

Did you like the way they communicated with each other? Do you like where it has left their relationship today? If not, be mindful or those same words will come out when you talk to your spouse—and they will lead to the same results. The creative force of words cannot be overestimated.

## THREE TRUTHS ABOUT WORDS

To start changing things for the better, we first need to recognize three essential truths about the nature of words. If we can begin to work these truths into our thinking, they will help us steer away from words that bring death and toward words that create life. We'll explore each of these truths in more detail in the pages ahead, but here's a brief overview.

### 1. WORDS ARE A GIFT FROM GOD.

The ability to use words at all is a gift that has been given to us by our Creator. As such, we have a responsibility to use our words well. As we've seen, God was the first one to harness the creative force of words—and he has entrusted us with the same ability to use words to create the world around us. Given the substantial nature of this gift, we can't just throw our words around any old way we please; they contain too much power. The only acceptable response to the gift we've been given is to show respect to the Giver by using it well.

Imagine if someone you love were to pull you aside one day and hand you $10,000, saying, "Hey, this is my gift to you, free and clear. I want you to use it to create a better life for yourself and to help make life better for others." You would be intentional about how you spent that money, right? You wouldn't go out and blow it on worthless junk. You would be careful to spend it wisely, squeezing all the possible good out of it. Well, believe it or not, our words are infinitely more important in shaping our lives than any amount of money—and they have been given to us with those exact instructions: use this power to create a better life for yourself and to help make life better for others. With that gift comes responsibility. Jesus's disciple Luke wrote in his gospel:

> When someone has been given much, much will be required in return; and when someone has been entrusted with much, even more will be required. (12:48)

## 2. WORDS CAN BUILD UP OR TEAR DOWN.

As a kid, you probably chanted the phrase "Sticks and stones may break my bones, but words will never hurt me." I know I did. With a little age and experience, we come to realize that even though it sounds good in theory, the phrase is just plain wrong. Words *can* hurt. I bet you don't have any problem remembering the last harsh words that were spoken to you or the last encouraging words you received. Other people's words can have an incredible impact on us, whether we want them to or not. They have the ability to create the atmosphere of our lives. They also have the ability to create atmosphere for others.

Not long ago, while I was boarding a flight from Los Angeles to New York, I got an unwelcomed reminder about the potential words have to create an air of negativity. I had just put my bag in the overhead compartment and was settling into the aisle seat I had booked weeks in advance when a burly guy walked up to me and huffed, "You're in my seat!" I pulled out my boarding pass and double-checked it. I was in the right seat—but that didn't make any difference to him. This guy was adamant. Getting angrier by the minute, he used a few choice words to tell me how stupid I was for sitting in his seat and how I needed to move out of the way so he could sit down.

About that time, a flight attendant realized what was going on and stepped in to settle things. She looked at our boarding passes, which, sure enough, both indicated the same seat number. But there was one major difference: my accuser's ticket was for a flight to San Francisco, not to New York. He had boarded the wrong airplane. As you can imagine, he didn't take the embarrassment well. Barreling back down the aisle toward the exit, he berated the attendants for allowing him to get on the wrong flight and spewed venom about how he would be filing a complaint with the airline's management.

As I sat back down, I began to notice how the energy around me had changed. One man's thoughtless, angry words had dispersed a negative cloud over everyone in my section of the plane. The flight attendants were rattled, and my own blood pressure was skyrocketing. Mr. San Francisco had left me feeling disjointed and defensive. Because he had chosen to dole out massive negativity and criticism over what could have been a simple, easily addressed misunderstanding, he tore the entire atmosphere around him down, along with everyone within it. With his words, he shifted everyone's reality.

## 3. THE QUALITY OF YOUR LIFE IS DETERMINED BY THE QUALITY OF YOUR WORDS.

The way you choose to communicate will ultimately affect every area of your life. Words aren't neutral. Every word that goes out has a consequence attached to it. How you speak to your friends, family members, and coworkers will determine the quality of those relationships. The same is true in your spiritual life. How well you communicate with God through prayer will determine the quality of your connection with him. Your internal dialogue with yourself will determine the quality of your actions and interactions each day. When you consider all these things together, it naturally follows that the quality of your very life is determined by the words you speak. Being able to express yourself effectively is crucial to living the life you've imagined.

I recently came across a study conducted by linguistic researchers on a large cross section of violent prisoners.[3] The researchers met with the prisoners and studied the range and type of vocabulary they used. They determined that these prisoners had about one-fifth the vocabulary of the average person in America, noting that one of the major contributing factors to the violent histories of the men was that they had no other way to express themselves. What a clear example of how the ability to use words—or in this case, the *inability* to use words—determines the quality of life itself.

## WORDS OF POWER

Remember the sociologists who set out to determine the most powerful four-word phrase, three-word phrase, and two-word phrase, and the single most powerful word in the English language? *Once upon a time* took the four-word distinction with good reason, as we've seen. The other winners probably won't come as much of a shock, but lest I leave you hanging, here they are:

> Most Powerful Three-Word Phrase: *I love you*
> Most Powerful Two-Word Phrase: *I'm sorry*
> Most Powerful Single Word: *I*

Not surprised? That's because you already know that the phrases *I love you* and *I'm sorry* and the word *I* are filled with immense power. Something within you instinctively recognizes their significance. But the truth is that all of our words are just as significant; we simply don't treat them as such.

Once you and I become aware of the inherent power words carry, we have to do something with that knowledge. As the old adage goes, "To know and not to do is really not to know." So what can we do? It all begins with being intentional. We have to be intentional about harnessing what comes out of our mouths, not only for our benefit but also for the benefit of others and for God's glory. The best way to get started down this path is to discover and adopt what I like to call a "tongue-pierced lifestyle."

## CHOOSING A *TONGUE-PIERCED* LIFESTYLE

Throughout these pages, we'll be discussing what it looks like to live a tongue-pierced lifestyle—that is, a lifestyle that acknowledges the importance of using your words to love God and love others. The words that exemplify a tongue-pierced lifestyle are words that reflect a heart filled with love—words that will impact your reality in ways that will bring you the meaning, relationships, and success you want. When you begin to live a tongue-pierced lifestyle, you will finally be able to move toward the life you were created for. But getting there requires making the decision to become intentional about the words you speak.

This doesn't mean you have to become a hypervigilant, politician-like communicator who weighs and stresses over every word you utter. We are talking about life in the real world, after all. Being intentional simply means refusing to be careless with your language any longer and becoming more conscientious of how you talk to yourself and the people around you so you can have a positive impact on your own life and on theirs.

What would it look like if you committed to choosing a tongue-pierced lifestyle? What if you began focusing on using only words that lead to life and build others up? What would it look like if everyone in your family decided to do the same? How about if everyone in your office started using words that showed love toward others? What if the people in your social circles, in your church, and in your community began intentionally choosing words that promoted life instead of allowing negativity, complaining, gossip, and other deadly words to slip in? The results would be nothing short of revolutionary. You can be the catalyst. As you dive into the pages ahead, I invite you—I challenge you, even—to commit to transforming your life by changing the words you speak. Are you ready?

*Chapter 2*

# WHAT YOUR WORDS SAY ABOUT YOU

*Words are the voice of the heart.*

Confucius

*The words you speak come from the heart.*

Jesus (Matt. 15:18)

One night, during the time I was preparing to write this book, I got sucked into one of the ubiquitous cop dramas that seem to dominate television. As I sat in my living room watching the disgruntled perpetrator get cuffed and thrown into the back of a police car, the Miranda rights being recited to him struck me in a new way: "You have the right to remain silent. Anything you say can and will be held against you." Of course, I'd heard those words many times before in television shows and movies, but I had never really thought about the implication they have for all of us. They aren't just true for alleged criminals; most of what you and I say can and will be held against us at some point too.

How often have you made judgments about other people based on what they say? You may not want to admit it, but I'm sure you do it every single day. We all do. Right or wrong, we make a number of assumptions based on people's vocabulary, their tonality, whether their words are positive or negative, and whether they seem self-focused or others-focused. When we don't know a person well, everything that comes out of his or her mouth helps to shape the impression we are forming. Of course, the way we perceive other people and the way they perceive us depends on a number of conscious and subconscious factors, but the use of words ranks high on the list. Blame it on human nature.

Before you begin to feel bad about assessing people based on something you may initially consider superficial, let me assure you of two things:

> 1. They're doing the same thing to you; they can't help it any more than you can.
> 2. Assessments based on words are not as superficial as you may think.

When you make judgment calls about people based on what they say (or when they do the same to you), you are actually keying into something much deeper. The words you are reacting to serve as tiny windows, allowing you to see what lies at the center of their being. In reality, you are responding to their heart. As Jesus himself said, "The words you speak come from the heart" (Matt. 15:18).

Words are so much more than sounds and syllables; they are little reflections of the condition of your being. As such, word problems are not just word problems; they are heart problems. Whatever rules your heart will determine the words you speak and as a result, the direction and quality of your life.

# THE PRINCIPLE OF ORGANIC CONSISTENCY

Words are a gift from God, reflect the condition of your heart, and have the power to direct your entire life, so it makes sense that the Bible has a lot to say about them. In fact, there are over four hundred verses in Scripture that relate directly to words, focusing on everything from their origin to their inherent creative force, to how we should harness them. (For a complete list of these verses, go to TonguePierced.com.)

There's no getting around the Bible's primary assertion that there is a direct correlation between the things you say and the state of your heart. If your heart is filled with bitterness or impurity, you are going to speak bitter and impure words. If your heart is full of love, you are going to speak encouraging, empowering words. Your words reveal what lies deep inside you, whether you want them to or not.

When I was growing up, my family owned a small duplex property near our home. We rented it out on an annual basis. I have vivid memories of going with my mother to clean up and refurbish that duplex after each tenant moved out, in preparation for the next one to move in. The thing I remember most about the property was the apple tree in the front yard. As a kid, I loved jumping up and picking the apples. The only problem was that the tree didn't produce very good apples. Every once in a while, I would get a few that were okay to eat, but for the most part they were small, hard, and sour.

I'm no apple tree arborist, but I know enough to know why those apples were no good—the tree wasn't healthy. Whether the problem was in the soil or in the roots of the tree itself, I have no idea. But I do know that my little apple tree was only capable of producing fruit consistent with its core level of well-being. No matter how much I wished the tree would give me deliciously plump, juicy apples, it simply didn't have what it needed to produce them. Even though I didn't know it at the time, the principle of organic consistency was at work here. Whatever seed and soil a fruit springs from will determine the quality of that fruit.

The same principle applies to your words. Thanks to the principle of organic consistency, you will never be successful using your words to positively impact your own life and the lives of others simply by trying to edit what comes out of your mouth. You have to get to the root of your word problems—the condition of your heart. Superficial techniques and quick fixes will only get you so far. To really change your life by changing your words, it's essential to examine the source of your speech habits.

## THE HEART OF THE MATTER

During Jesus's earthly ministry, the religious leaders of the day, the Pharisees, were always trying to trip him up. They would ask convoluted questions to try to catch him in an inconsistency. In one of these attempts, a Pharisee approached Jesus and tried to trap him by asking him to pick the greatest commandment in all of Scripture. Without hesitation, Jesus replied,

> "You must love the LORD your God with all your
> heart, all your soul, and all your mind." This is
> the first and greatest commandment. A second is

equally important: "Love your neighbor as yourself." (Matt. 22:37–39)

According to Jesus, the greatest call on our lives is to love God
with everything we are and to love those around us as much as we
love ourselves. Sounds like a tall order, doesn't it? How can we hope
to accomplish those two things? Well, since words are the primary
way we relate to and communicate with each other, it follows that we
should begin with our everyday conversations. We can choose to consistently speak words that bring life rather than death, words of love,
encouragement, comfort, and celebration instead of words of criticism, gossip, complaining, and hate. Of course, anyone—Christian
or otherwise, with the goal of loving God and others or simply with
the goal of improving his or her own life—can make a decision of the
will to focus on positive, life-giving words, but that individual won't
be successful for very long if those words aren't organically consistent
with the condition of his or her heart.

Imagine there is a driver's seat positioned right smack in the
middle of your heart. Most of your life is a competition over who
is sitting in that seat. Sometimes it's going to be you. Other times it
may feel like one of your parents, your spouse, a close friend, or even
your boss is trying to slide in. Whoever sits in that seat at the center
of your being controls you. Conventional wisdom would argue that
you should be the seat's sole occupant, that you shouldn't allow anything or anyone else to direct your heart. In fact, that's how we all
think at some point in our lives.

But if you have decided to follow Jesus, you know that becoming
a Christian changes your perspective. Suddenly you realize that life is

about more than you and your own agenda, that God's purposes for you are more substantial than anything you've imagined for yourself. The realization makes you want to get out of the driver's seat and let God settle in. When you do, his love begins to change your heart, revitalizing your whole being from the inside out.

Since your words are the outward indication of what's going on internally, they reveal who is sitting in the driver's seat. They are like a neon sign broadcasting whether you are living a self-focused life or a God-directed life. They scream out how you feel about yourself and others and tell people exactly what's important to you. Look at Jesus's answer again:

> "You must love the LORD your God with all your heart, all your soul, and all your mind." This is the first and greatest commandment. A second is equally important: "Love your neighbor as yourself." (Matt. 22:37–39)

The catch is that it's impossible to love your neighbor as yourself unless you are consumed with loving God and receiving his love in return. You can only express love to the degree you have experienced it. As Paul David Tripp wrote,

> It is only when I love God above all else that I will love my neighbor as myself. It's only when God is in the rightful place in my life that I will treat you with the love that I have received from him.… [That's why you can't] fix language problems,

communication problems, and word problems horizontally; you first fix them vertically.[1]

Trying to use your words to love God, others, and yourself fully out of a heart that has never known the fullness of God's redeeming love is nothing short of frustrating. But if you allow Jesus to take up residence in the center of your being, the words that bring abundant life will become the natural by-product of your God-focused heart.

## AN ONGOING BATTLE

Still, no one should make the mistake of thinking that Christians suddenly have it all together in the words arena. If you are a Christian or if you know any Christians, you can attest to this fact. Golden apples don't start falling from your mouth simply because you choose to follow Jesus. Yes, once you become a Christian, you are a new creation in Christ (see 2 Cor. 5:17), but on this side of heaven, there is and always will be an ongoing, daily struggle with the flesh. As the apostle Paul wrote in his letter to believers in the Galatian church,

> The sinful nature wants to do evil, which is just the opposite of what the Spirit wants. And the Spirit gives us desires that are the opposite of what the sinful nature desires. These two forces are constantly fighting each other. (Gal. 5:17)

Even as a follower of Jesus, part of you will still want to control the driver's seat in your heart. Sometimes you may find yourself just trying to perch on the edge of the seat. Other times, convinced you know what's best, you may start trying to nudge God over so you can get your hands on the wheel. If you take control back completely, you'll probably end up facing some form of destruction and pain—which will just make you want to turn things back over to him, that is, until you feel the need to perch on the edge of the seat again. As long as you and I are alive, we will be engaged in an ongoing battle with our human nature.

Think of your words as a gauge that lets you know where you are in the ongoing battle. When you hear your words becoming harsh, coarse, and negative, you are edging God out of the driver's seat, focusing on yourself and your needs. But when your words are full of love, encouragement, and praise, it's a good sign that God is in his rightful position, steering you toward his purposes.

James penned some of the most powerful thoughts in Scripture about this struggle as it relates to controlling the tongue:

> For if we could control our tongues, we would be perfect and could also control ourselves in every other way.
>
> We can make a large horse go wherever we want by means of a small bit in its mouth. And a small rudder makes a huge ship turn wherever the pilot chooses to go, even though the winds are strong. In the same way, the tongue is a small thing that makes grand speeches.
>
> But a tiny spark can set a great forest on fire. And the tongue is a flame of fire. It is a whole world

of wickedness, corrupting your entire body. It can set your whole life on fire, for it is set on fire by hell itself.

People can tame all kinds of animals, birds, reptiles, and fish, but no one can tame the tongue. *It is restless and evil, full of deadly poison. Sometimes it praises our Lord and Father, and sometimes it curses those who have been made in the image of God. And so blessing and cursing come pouring out of the same mouth.* Surely, my brothers and sisters, this is not right! Does a spring of water bubble out with both fresh water and bitter water? (3:2–11)

If the tongue projects the thoughts and intentions of the heart—and can be full of such evil, cursing, and deadly poison—it follows that a heart not centered on God is full of the same. Not to mention, a tongue that has been bridled, as James puts it, is the indication of a heart that is allowing God's love to fill it and move it toward a higher level of spiritual maturity. The battle over your words—and your life—rages on every day. Every time you speak, you choose a side. Judging by the kind of words you've used in the last few days, which side are you allowing to win?

## CHOOSING SIDES

On one side, you can choose to use words of praise and encourage-ment or make the wise decision to hold your tongue completely. On the other side, you can choose destruction by gossiping, complaining, and cursing, to name a few negative options. Let's take a quick look at these specific choices on either side of the battle line. We'll dive into them more deeply in the pages ahead.

## PRAISE

Praise sounds like a lofty endeavor, doesn't it? Really, it's simply thanking God for who he is. Words of praise reflect a God-focused heart. They demand a shift of attention away from selfishness and toward God's goodness and love, which will automatically influence everything that comes out of your mouth. Too often, you and I fall into the trap of only praising God when we're inside a church building on Sunday morning. But if we are going to win the battle over the tongue, we need to make a practice of praising him every day. David wrote in Psalm 145:2, "I will praise you every day; yes, I will praise you forever."

One of the most practical ways to do this is to create a habit of starting your day with praise. The first hour of your day is similar to the bit in a horse's mouth or the rudder on a ship. If you choose to begin your day with positive words of praise to God, the rest of your day will be better for it. You'll be in a better place when evening comes. So think about it: What are the first words that come out of your mouth when you wake up? Are you willing to start replacing those words with words of gratitude and thanksgiving?

Begin by thanking God for who he is. Think about his attributes and how they affect your life. Thank him for his love, his blessings, his direction, his forgiveness, and his peace. Let those words settle into your heart and become part of the wellspring you'll speak from for the rest of the day. Bringing your tongue—and thereby your life—under control begins with the simple habit of praise.

## ENCOURAGEMENT

Every person you walk by on the street or pass at the bank or stand beside in the grocery store line may as well be wearing an invisible sign that reads, "Encourage me." All people need encouragement, even if they don't want to admit it. In fact, it's usually the ones who won't admit it—the ones who walk around with the biggest scowls on their faces—who need encouragement the most. And you have the ability to give them exactly what they need. As you begin speaking from a God-focused heart, encouraging words will come naturally. You will begin seeing other people as God sees them, which will make you want to encourage them to grow in that direction.

One of my favorite quotations comes from Goethe and speaks to this truth:

> If you treat an individual as he is, he will remain how he is. But if you treat him as if he were what he ought to be and could be, he will become what he ought to be and could be.

That is the essence of encouragement—treating the people in your life as the best possible versions of themselves, whether they are currently living up to that standard or not.

What if you practiced speaking encouragement to your spouse, your children, or your friends? Instead of focusing on what they do wrong and nitpicking their faults, what if you started treating them as if they already were all they could be? What if your words grew out of the vision of their fulfilled potential instead of their current reality? You would begin to see them grow and flourish in ways you never imagined. Those are the kind of words that have the power to affect people for a lifetime. Trust me, the people in your life already know what their problems and weaknesses are; they don't need you to tell them. When you become a source of encouragement to them rather than a faultfinder and self-appointed problem-fixer, you are cooperating with God in building them into who he wants them to be.

## HOLDING YOUR TONGUE

Do you know anyone who talks too much? Of course you do. I bet a name or two popped to mind immediately. Here's something to consider: Would your name pop to someone else's mind in answer to that question? Could you be accused of running off at the mouth a little too often? Sometimes your best use of language happens when you say nothing at all. There's immense wisdom in keeping quiet at the right times. After all, God gave us one mouth and two ears for a reason. We're probably safe to assume that he wants us to listen twice as much as we speak.

Learning to hold your tongue requires a degree of humility; it takes a realization that your opinion may not be the best or most important one in the room. Often it means letting go of your need to be right. As King Solomon wrote,

> Fools think their own way is right, but the wise listen to others. (Prov. 12:15)

Sometimes we are so busy explaining, proving, and justifying ourselves and our opinions that we forget to listen. As a result, we miss out on the insight of others—insight that may be extremely beneficial to us. Solomon continued,

> The wise don't make a show of their knowledge, but
> fools broadcast their foolishness. (Prov. 12:23)

Consider these two verses taken together: Wise people listen to others and don't flaunt the knowledge they have, while fools think they are right and broadcast their foolishness to everyone around them. I don't know about you, but I would rather be found among the wise.

> We are masters of the unsaid words, but slaves of those we let slip out.
>
> Winston Churchill

Learning to hold your tongue when everything in you wants to speak takes practice, not to mention maturity. But again, awareness is key. Start paying attention to your own mouth. Try to be more cognizant of when you should stop talking. Don't let your tongue be your master; choose to master it instead.

On the opposite side of the battle, there are three major categories of words that can sabotage us. These words are actually like small, daily doses of poison—over time they result in death.

## *GOSSIP*

Gossip, in all its forms, is inherently destructive. While it can creep into our conversations under a lot of guises, there are two main manifestations:

> **1. Spreading lies about another person.** Most of the time when people talk about someone behind his or her back, they don't even know if what they are saying is true—and it's usually not. They are likely just repeating what they have heard someone else say. By jumping on the bandwagon of gossip, they add to the proliferation of misinformation and hurtful lies.

> **2. Discussing someone's problems with anyone other than that person.** Many people become convinced that they are actually doing good by talking among themselves about the negative circumstances in a third party's life. They hide behind the excuse that they are concerned and say they want to help make things better, when all they are really doing is gaining subversive pleasure by gossiping about what someone else is struggling with.

Gossip is a sin, plain and simple. Not only does it tear people down, but it also deteriorates trust. But here's the thing most gossips don't realize: while gossip is hurtful to those who are being gossiped about, it hurts the gossiper just as much, if not more. Those poisonous words seep into the soul and create toxicity from the outside in. King Solomon wasn't silent on this issue either:

> The words of a gossip are like choice morsels; they
> go down to the inmost parts. (Prov. 18:8 NIV)

They go down with some immediate satisfaction, but in short order they start causing pain—as is the case with most sin. It's impossible to gossip about someone else without being personally affected in a negative way.

## COMPLAINTS

How often do you catch yourself complaining about your boss's attitude, your kids' behavior, your friends' neediness, your overcrowded schedule, your constant aches and pains? The list could go on and on. Most people love to complain, so much so that it gets turned into a competition. At one point or another, I bet you have said something like, "You think your day was bad; wait until you hear about mine" or "Your son sounds like an angel compared to mine lately."

For some reason, we have bought into the idea that complaining about our difficulties will make us feel better, even if only by getting us a little sympathy. But complaining isn't an end in itself; it's actually the catalyst for a vicious cycle. When we get attention or comfort by complaining about one thing, we're more likely to start complaining about something else. We start complaining a little more often. Before long, those complaints become self-fulfilling prophecies. What may have begun as a small irritation grows into a more substantial problem because we have continued to feed it with words, words, and more words.

Truth is, no one likes a complainer. After a while, other people will start tuning you out. The problem is that you can't tune yourself out. Your inner ear is paying close attention to every word you say and your subconscious is working to reinforce each one's truth. The more you talk about your struggles, the more strength you give them. As they gain strength, you'll want to talk about them even more—and the vicious cycle ensues. That's why, in his letter to the Philippian church, Paul wrote, "Do everything without complaining and arguing" (Phil. 2:14).

Paul understood that complaining never leads to anything positive but only to more trouble and more difficult situations. While we should never remain quiet about true mistreatment or injustices, complaining about every little thing that's wrong in our lives will do nothing but perpetuate our problems.

## CURSING

One of the single most effective ways to harness your words and use them to love God and love others is to be intentional about removing all curse words from your speech. Is cursing something you've struggled with? You don't have to be ashamed to admit it. Like most of our language patterns, cursing is largely a learned behavior.

I grew up around people who turned cursing into something of an art form. Needless to say, that impacted the way I viewed and used curse words. As a teenager, I did my best to match wits with these stellar examples. When I began to realize that cursing probably wasn't the best and highest use of my words, I started trying to curb my affinity for it. Unfortunately, by that time it had become a habit—and habits can be difficult to break.

Like both gossip and complaining, cursing is a slow poison that drips into the core of your being as you practice it day in and day out. Curse words even have the inherent power to keep you at a distance from God. Conversely, the absence of cursing can be a sign that God is working in your life. If you are walking closely with God and he is sitting in the driver's seat of your life, curse words just won't feel right in your mouth.

I recently read about a revival that happened in America in 1904. Apparently, a move of God swept the nation that year, and people came to faith in Jesus in droves. Examining how the revival affected a group of coal miners in one particular mining town, the author observed,

> Stoppages occurred in coal mines, not due to unpleasantness between management and workers, but because so many foulmouthed miners became converted and stopped using foul language that the horses which hauled the coal trucks in the mines could no longer understand what was being said to them, and transportation ground to a halt.[2]

When these coal miners surrendered themselves to Jesus, their words began to spring from a different source. As a result, their speech changed so drastically that their horses couldn't even understand them. Now, I'm sure they still struggled with the habit from

time to time, but I admire how immediately and fully they understood the connection between their words and their hearts and chose
to harness their language.

## WHAT LIES WITHIN

If I were to record your words over the next few days, what would
they tell me about the condition of your heart? What would they tell
me about what's going on inside you? Would they tell me that you
are filled with love and that you express that love fully to God and
to the people around you? That you are more interested in the well-
being of those you care about than your own? Or would they reflect
selfishness, discontentedness, fear, and anger? Would they show that
you are eager to get other people to do and say the things you need
them to do and say, regardless of the language you have to use to
make that happen? Maybe I would find the source of some crippling
insecurity in the way you put yourself down and beat yourself up for
every mistake you make.

Here's one thing I know: That recording would tell me everything I could ever want to learn about the state of your inner
being. Just like the apples on that old apple tree, your words are
the inescapable evidence of the health of the soil in which they
grow. What kind of verbal fruit are you producing? As James went
on to say,

> Does a fig tree produce olives, or a grapevine pro-
> duce figs? No, and you can't draw fresh water from
> a salty spring. (3:12)

Before moving into the chapters ahead, let me encourage you to take some time to deeply consider the following question: What are your words saying about you? As we've established, awareness and intentionality are key to changing your habits of speech for the better. Over the next week or two, make an intentional effort to listen to what comes out of your mouth. Listen to how it sounds. Note how it affects the people around you. Do your words build up or tear down? Are they moving in the direction of life or in the direction of death?

Chapter 3

# THE MOST IMPORTANT CONVERSATIONS YOU'LL EVER HAVE

*It is better in prayer to have a heart without
words than words without a heart.*

Gandhi

*Then you will call on me and come and pray to me,
and I will listen to you. You will seek me and find
me when you seek me with all your heart.*

Jeremiah 29:12–13 NIV

Sometimes when my wife and I are talking with another person or another couple, I'll notice that we have a tendency to say the same thing, in the same way, at the same time. For example, if someone is telling a story, we often interject an "uh-huh" at the same time or react with the same phrase when the story is over. As scary as that may sound, it's completely natural. When you spend as much time with another person as my wife and I spend together, you begin to pick up their words, their phrasing, and even their tonality. Early on in a close relationship, you may find yourself using words that you've never used before simply because the person you've been spending so much time with uses them. They get in your ear, and it doesn't take long to start adopting them as your own.

This reality goes a long way toward proving an old maxim: You are the same today as you'll be in five years except for two things—the people you associate with and the books you read. What you allow into your mind is critical to your ongoing growth and development. You become like the people you spend the most time with. Who you talk to the most influences what you say when you talk to yourself and to others. As such, you should be extremely choosy about who your most frequent conversations are with. Those conversations—whether they are with a spouse, a close friend, or a coworker—will greatly influence your words … and therefore your life.

Given the weight of this truth, let me propose an idea for you to consider: What if the person you talked to the most was God? What if, as you moved through your day, you were engaged in an ongoing dialogue with him? Not in a weird, kneel down in the lunch line kind of way, but rather in simple, quiet thoughts directed toward him and an intentional focus on hearing what he might want to say to you in return. Or to put it another way: What if you engaged in ongoing prayer? Those conversations with God would begin to shape the way you think, the way you speak to yourself, and the way you communicate with the people in your world.

Prayer isn't complicated. It is simply talking with God, using your words to connect with him, telling him what's going on with you, and being quiet long enough to hear from him. When you make spending time in communication with God a habit, you'll begin to think like he thinks. When that happens, the words that come out of your mouth will start to sound more like his words.

The time you spend with him will begin to have an effect on you, just as any ongoing influence does. And what better influence to be affected by? Prayer really works. It not only changes circumstances, but it also changes you along the way.

A few years ago, a well-renowned cardiologist at Duke University Medical Center became intrigued by the notion of prayer's ability to alter outcomes and decided to do an experiment on his heart patients. He set out asking the question, "Is there a measurable incremental benefit to prayer?" After the experiment ended, the doctor concluded,

> We saw impressive reductions in all of the negative outcomes—the bad outcomes that were measured in the study. What we look for routinely in cardiology trials are outcomes such as death, a heart attack, or the lungs filling with water—what we call congestive heart failure—in patients who are treated in the course of these problems. In the group randomly assigned to prayer therapy, there was a 50 percent reduction in all complications and a 100 percent reduction in major complications.[1]

In an unrelated study, a physician at the Pacific College of Medicine in San Francisco set out to test the effect of prayer on advanced AIDS patients. Her conclusions were similar. She found that the patients who received prayer had six times fewer hospitalizations, and those hospitalizations were significantly shorter than the people who received no prayer. She said in an interview,

I was sort of shocked. In a way, it's like witnessing a
miracle. There was no way to understand this from
my experience and from my basic understanding
of science.[2]

When asked to comment on these and other similar medical
studies, Chuck Colson, a prominent Christian observer of culture,
said,

Such studies have plenty of critics, but the new
research has left many scratching their heads. Is
prayer something that can be put under a micro-
scope and examined? Probably not, but one thing's
for sure: prayer works, and prayer is real.[3]

Though science will likely never be able to define exactly what
happens in our conversations with God, one thing is for sure—when
we talk, he hears what we say.

## TALKING WITH GOD

Stop and think about the incredible privilege of prayer for a minute.
You have the ability to talk to God—the Author of the world, your
Creator—whenever and wherever you want to. You don't have to
know a secret code, use any particular phrasing, or go through a
priest. You can communicate with God anytime. He is ready and
willing to engage in conversation with you. In fact, he wants you to
make talking to him a regular part of your day. As Paul wrote,

> Devote yourselves to prayer with an alert mind and
> a thankful heart. (Col. 4:2)

Immersing yourself in conversation with God does three major things in your life, all of which act as catalysts for shaping your words and directing the way you use them. First of all, when you talk to God, you acknowledge his existence. Second, you connect with him on a deeper level. And third, you demonstrate your dependence on him as your source.

## 1. ACKNOWLEDGE THAT GOD EXISTS.

When you pray, you demonstrate your belief in God's existence. More than 90 percent of Americans say they believe God is real.[4] Out of the 90 percent, one-third pray several times a day,[5] proving what they say they believe. To them, God isn't just a concept or a question mark. He is an actual being with whom they can engage. Their actions give credence to their belief and acknowledge the tangible existence of God.

Interestingly, the 10 percent who say they don't believe in God help to prove his existence just as powerfully as those who engage in regular prayer. While they may spend decades in vehement debates trying to disprove the existence of a higher power (atheists) or contending that there's no way to know if there is a God (agnostics), self-proclaimed nonbelievers are quick to pray to the one they disavow when tragedy strikes. As the old saying goes, "There are no atheists in foxholes." When the temporal is in turmoil, something inside every human being cries out for the eternal. We are wired for a connection with the one who created us. Even those who won't acknowledge him in everyday situations turn to him when the dark nights come, thereby powerfully attesting to his existence.

## 2. CONNECT WITH GOD ON A DEEPER LEVEL.

Your relationship with God, if you are a Christian, is a bit like your relationship with your spouse, if you are married. On your wedding day, you stood in front of your family and friends and made a lifelong commitment to the person you love. You and your husband- or wife-to-be recited vows, pledging to honor and cherish each other, had some cake, and then embarked on your new life together. But then what? Did you stop talking to each other after the wedding was over? Of course not. If you had, your marriage would have crumbled more quickly than that cake. Instead, you started engaging in the ongoing conversation that creates life. You began using your words to connect with your spouse, growing and strengthening your partnership day in and day out.

So it is with God. Your initial connection with God happens when you submit your life to him, when you allow him to move into that driver's seat at the core of your being and take control. But that connection is just the beginning. God wants to continually deepen the relationship as you choose to engage him in conversation with daily prayer. Your words have the ability to move you into his presence and to put you in a position to be able to hear what he wants to say to you.

You can't have a deep relationship with someone you don't talk to—something you know to be true when it comes to your earthly family and friends. If you went for a couple of months without having real conversation with your spouse, a parent, or a friend, the relationship would suffer. You wouldn't feel the same closeness with that person as you would if you had been making frequent, regular investments in the relationship. Why should it be any different in your relationship with God?

## 3. DEMONSTRATE YOUR DEPENDENCE UPON GOD.

I have an engineer friend who, as part of his job, regularly oversees the development of large residential buildings in different parts of the country. Every time he starts a new project, he spends an incredible amount of time with the architect who designed the building. They go over plans and blueprints together ad nauseam. There's no way my friend would set out on a new building project without being crystal clear on what the designer had in mind. That would be crazy. If he failed to follow the blueprints of the person with the complete vision for the job, disaster would be right around the corner.

Even so, that's how millions of people go about building their lives. They forge ahead with what they think is in their best interest, neglecting to consult the one who has the blueprint. But there's no reason to barrel ahead blindly. By choosing to talk with God every day, you place yourself in a position where he can show you the best possible plan for your life and give you what you need to live it out.

Let me be clear, though: Prayer is not ultimately about God being available to you. It's about you being available to God; it's about letting him know that you are ready and willing for him to shape your life. As you admit your dependence on him and acknowledge that his plan is bigger and better than your own, you open the door for him to work in your life. Some of the most powerful, most life-transforming words you can ever speak are, "God, I need you. Please show me the path you want me to walk." God won't force himself on you, but if you'll engage in the conversation, he'll be sure to carry his end of it.

## SOMETHING TO TALK ABOUT

Don't you hate when you are trying to talk to someone but you don't really have anything to say? Or when you stumble into one of those awkward lulls in the conversation so big it could swallow a house? Some people never have that problem, but for those of you who are a little more introverted like me, I'm sure you can relate.

Over the years, I've heard a lot of people admit that this is their hang-up with talking to God—they just don't know where to begin. A loss of words with God stems from an incorrect view of who he is and what he expects from us. We get stagnated when we feel like we need to impress him or feel that we can't be ourselves—but neither of those things should apply to our conversations with the one who created us. He already knows everything about us, so there's no reason to approach him with anything other than complete transparency. As David wrote,

> You have searched me, LORD, and you know me.
> You know when I sit and when I rise; you perceive
> my thoughts from afar. You discern my going out
> and my lying down; you are familiar with all my
> ways. Before a word is on my tongue you, LORD,
> know it completely. (Ps. 139:1–4 NIV)

Teaching a group of disciples how to pray, Jesus emphasized that we don't have to approach God with anything other than who we are. God doesn't want us to come to him putting on airs, using high, theological language, and trying to talk about things we aren't really interested in. He is simply looking for an earnest conversation:

> When you pray, don't be like the hypocrites who love to pray publicly on street corners and in the synagogues where everyone can see them. I tell you the truth, that is all the reward they will ever get. But when you pray, go away by yourself, shut the door behind you, and pray to your Father in private. (Matt. 6:5–6)

Remember the Pharisees I mentioned in the last chapter—the religious leaders who were always trying to trip Jesus up? They would often stand on street corners and say long, eloquent prayers as people passed. They wanted to look pious, but as Jesus points out, they were far from it. They weren't really talking to God; they were just play-acting. He goes so far as to call them "hypocrites." Their prayers had nothing to do with engaging in conversation but were more about how they were perceived by the people walking by. That's the opposite of how you and I should pray.

God wants us to come to him simply. Our conversations with him are to be private, not for show. He wants us to talk to him as we would a trusted friend, to get to know him better so he can rub off on us. Once we come to that realization, we can get down to the business of being ourselves and having open, honest conversations with God about the things that matter in our world—namely, ourselves and others.

## PRAYING FOR YOURSELF

Speaking of honesty, I bet the first thing you pray for is not usually world peace or provision for the needy in your community. If you are like most people, it's not even your family or friends. Most of us are inclined to pray for our own needs before praying for other people or larger-scale issues. See if you can relate to this scenario: It's five minutes before a big presentation, an important test, or a major event, and you find yourself praying, *Oh, God, please help me do well. This is such a big deal, and it really needs to be great. If you could just supernaturally intervene right now and pull all the pieces together, I would be grateful.* Then, as an afterthought, you may include, *Oh, and help those who need you around the world, and be with my brother while he travels. Amen.* Does that kind of prayer resonate?

If you tend to pray selfish prayers, you are not alone. Just as we like to talk about ourselves with others, we also like to talk about ourselves to God—what we want, what we need, what we think he can do to help us. And here's the good news: God is okay with those kinds of prayers. As David wrote,

> In the day when I cried out, You answered me, and
> made me bold with strength in my soul. (Ps. 138:3
> NKJV)

God wants you to come to him—to cry out—with every need, no matter how large or small. He will answer you. Now, it wouldn't be good if every one of your prayers sounded like the one above, but there's nothing wrong with praying for yourself. As you do, there are certain types of words you should focus on using. Go before God with words that are confident, bold, humble, and faith-filled all at the same time.

## CONFIDENT WORDS

God is for you. He loves you and wants to give you good things. He wants your life to have maximum impact and fulfillment. When you pray, pray with the confidence that comes along with that reality. Don't pray in a way that expects anything less than God's best. Know that your prayer will be heard and answered because you are his child. Look at what Jesus said:

> You parents—if your children ask for a loaf of bread, do you give them a stone instead? Or if they ask for a fish, do you give them a snake? Of course not! So if you sinful people know how to give good gifts to your children, how much more will your heavenly Father give good gifts to those who ask him. (Matt. 7:9–11)

Good parents build their children up and encourage them. They focus on their children's strengths rather than their faults and do their best to provide them with everything they need. In the same way, when God looks at you, he's not fixated on your flaws or focusing on your deficiencies. Rather, he's proud of you, fiercely protective of you, and focused on helping you live the abundant life he has in store. Why? Simply because he is your heavenly Father, and you are his child. When you are walking in that truth, you can approach your conversations with God with renewed confidence, knowing that he is for you and working everything together for your good.

## BOLD WORDS

Similarly, too many of us are inclined to pray meek, tentative prayers. We figure that what we have to say probably isn't important enough to bother God with; we assume he has more pressing issues at hand. But the Bible tells us over and over again that if we are followers of Jesus, we should pray boldly, expecting God to answer us. Jesus said it this way:

> You can ask me for anything in my name, and I will
> do it. (John 14:13)

Have you ever wondered why you have to ask God for the things you need? After all, if he knows everything about you, he already knows what you need. Why does he make you go through the process of asking? Just think about it: If God gave you everything you wanted or needed before you even asked, how would you know that the good things in your life were coming from him?

Often, when people stop talking with God regularly, they begin to see the circumstances in their lives that are actually blessings from God as random chance or luck. Sometimes they begin to take credit for the good they're experiencing; they miss the evidence of God's hand because they weren't talking to him about their needs and wants on the front end. But when you ask God for something specific and then that specific thing comes to pass, you know beyond the shadow of a doubt where it came from. God will get the glory, praise, and credit he deserves.

Praying boldly is simply praying with the aforementioned confidence that God hears your prayers and wants to bless you. Bold prayers garner big responses. As Jesus said,

> I tell you the truth, if you have faith and don't doubt, you can do things like this and much more. You can even say to this mountain, "May you be lifted up and thrown into the sea," and it will happen. You can pray for anything, and if you have faith, you will receive it. (Matt. 21:21–22)

Faith and doubt cannot coexist. So pray boldly for the job you are applying for. Pray boldly for the child you want to come into your marriage. Pray boldly for healing in the health situation you're dealing with. Pray boldly that God will bless you in the areas where you need blessing. No matter the situation or what you are praying for, use bold words. God will hear them and answer you accordingly.

## HUMBLE WORDS

At first glance, you may consider it contradictory to approach God with confident boldness and with humility at the same time, but there's no contradiction at all. Being humble before God simply means acknowledging that God is God and you are not. When you talk to him, use bold and confident words, but do so from a place of humility that is quick to submit to his ultimate will.

When a child comes to a parent and asks for something that isn't in her best interest, a loving parent will say no. Even if the child asks with confidence and boldness, the parent isn't going to honor a request that isn't good for her. The same is true with God. If you are praying for something that is outside of his will, he won't answer in the way you expect. With humility, trust that he knows more than you know; he sees farther than you can see.

Bold, confident prayers don't force God to do anything. They usher in his blessing when your requests are in line with his will for your life, but they don't manipulate him into giving you something that's out of alignment with his ultimate goals for you. The greater purpose of talking with God through prayer is to align your wants and needs with his will and desires. As you talk to God, his influence changes your heart to be more like his own, which in turn makes your words more reflective of his love. Let your posture as you talk with him demonstrate that knowledge.

## FAITH-FILLED WORDS

You cannot approach God with the confidence, boldness, and humility he desires if your conversations with him aren't rooted in a foundation of faith. He has promised to hear and answer the prayers of those who have placed their trust in him, but he has not promised the same to those yet to profess their belief. Sometimes he will answer the prayers of unbelievers for one of two reasons: (1) to bring glory to himself or (2) to help move that person toward a relationship with him. But he makes no promises to answer. There is one prayer, however, that God will always answer. That is the earnest prayer of someone choosing to put his or her faith in him for the first time.

## PRAYING FOR OTHERS

When we aren't talking to God about ourselves, we are usually talking to him about other people in our lives. Hopefully we are most often praying for them to do well and be well, for them to be strengthened and to fulfill their God-given potential. Other times, if we're honest, we are praying that God will change them to be more like we think they should be. Whatever your motivation in praying for others, there are a few reasons you should be doing it on a regular basis:

> **1. God says to pray for other people.** Part of loving others as yourself is being willing to go to God on their behalf, which takes both time and intentionality. Richard Foster, a modern-day philosopher on prayer, said, "If we truly love people, we will desire for them far more than is within our power to give them and this will lead us to prayer." Intercession gives you the ability to influence and bolster other people's lives in substantial ways.

> **2. Praying for other people grows your faith.** When you pray for someone and God answers that prayer, your faith increases.

**3. Praying for others strengthens relationships.**
Praying for someone draws you closer to that person. No matter where he or she is in the world—whether right next door to you or several continents away—you will feel more connected in the relationship because of your prayers.

**4. Praying for others impacts the world.** When you pray for another person, you are cooperating with God in helping that person become all that he or she is meant to be. You are playing an important part in raising that person up to impact the world.

But what, specifically, should you pray for when you pray for other people? There are two types of prayers for others that should be on your lips often—one comes very naturally, while the other takes more perspective and intentionality. When you pray for the people in your life, focus on speaking words of *safety* and words of *significance*.

## WORDS OF SAFETY

Concern over the day-to-day safety and well-being of family and friends is natural. Still, when it comes to praying that your mother has a safe flight or that your friend's doctor appointment goes well, you may be likely to think that God is too busy to be concerned— which can lead you to stop praying and simply hold your breath. Again, God is never too busy to hear your cries to him, no matter how big or small they may seem. He is concerned with what concerns you, which means he is more than willing to hear and answer prayers about the safety of those you love.

What does praying words of safety actually look like, practically speaking? First of all, you should pray for overall protection for your loved ones. Then, as part of that, pray specifically for what's going on with each one. Remember, when you pray specific prayers, you'll be able to see God answer those prayers and can celebrate accordingly. Maybe you pray for safe travels for a friend taking a long trip. Maybe you pray protection over a family member who is dealing with a chronic health issue. Perhaps your prayer is for a smooth recovery for someone you care about who has been sick recently. Or maybe your prayer is for your child's safety as he or she plays competitive sports. Whatever safety issues you are concerned about, take them to God. He will hear and answer your prayers.

## WORDS OF SIGNIFICANCE

Moving things up a notch, we should also be praying for significance for the people we love. That is, we should be praying that their lives will be filled with substance and meaning, that they will make a difference in the world, that God's purposes will be done through them.

If you study prayer in Scripture, the majority of prayers are more along these lines than they are focused on immediate concerns. In fact, Paul prayed some of the most powerful prayers of significance for others ever recorded. Take a look at this prayer for the believers in Ephesus:

> I have not stopped thanking God for you. I pray
> for you constantly, asking God, the glorious Father

of our Lord Jesus Christ, to give you spiritual wisdom and insight so that you might grow in your
knowledge of God. I pray that your hearts will be
flooded with light so that you can understand the
confident hope he has given to those he called—
his holy people who are his rich and glorious
inheritance.

I also pray that you will understand the incredible
greatness of God's power for us who believe him.
This is the same mighty power that raised Christ
from the dead and seated him in the place of honor
at God's right hand in the heavenly realms. (Eph.
1:16–20)

What a prayer! Can you imagine what would manifest in the
lives of those around you if you were praying that kind of prayer
over them every day? What would happen in your life if people
were praying such a prayer over you? The details of everyday life
often keep us so caught up in the mundane that we forget we have
access to the incredible resurrection power of Jesus within us. Even
as we pray for safe road trips and effective medical treatments, let's
not neglect to pray for *spiritual wisdom and insight* and that the
hearts of those we love will be *flooded with light* to *understand the
confident hope* God has given us. Pray for your loved ones to grow
closer to God, to be used by God, and to do God's will. Those are
powerful words that can change the lives of the people who are
most important to you.

If you will get into the practice of praying safety and significance over the people you love, not only will you be making a tangible difference in their lives, but you will also begin seeing subtle shifts in how you interact with them face-to-face. It's much harder to be harsh toward or critical of someone you are earnestly praying for. When you let your words toward others grow out of your heartfelt conversations with God about them, your relationships will be strengthened, and your family and friends will be influenced in ways you can only imagine.

## LISTEN UP

As you enter into conversations with God, take time to listen to what he has to say. Resist the urge to do all the talking. Just as in any conversation, there has to be give and take. Overtalking is one of the most common ways you and I block our ability to hear from God. Too often, our prayers go something like this:

> God, if you will just show me the path I should take, I will take it. You are so good, God. You have been good to me in the past. I want to honor you. Let me know what I should do next. I'm ready to hear from you. Amen.

Then we get up, walk away, and question why God didn't speak to us during our prayer time. You have to wonder if God is in heaven thinking, *I would love to tell you my will for your life, but I can't get a word in edgewise!*

If only we could learn to listen better—to practice the art of holding our tongue at the appropriate times, as mentioned in the last chapter—we would have deeper conversations with God. As David wrote, God wants us to "be still, and know that I am God!" (Ps. 46:10).

Being still in your conversations with God will allow you to get to know him more intimately, which has some practical benefits. Knowing God better draws you deeper into the abundant life Jesus promised (see John 10:10)—a life with more significance, greater impact, and clearer purpose.

## SHAPED BY ASSOCIATION

As you begin to spend more and more time with God, using your words as a means to connect with him and listening to what he wants to say to you, the more you will become like him. His influence will begin to rub off on you, and you will see the evidence of the time you're spending with him in the way you speak to yourself and to those around you. Your words will start to sound more like his words. They will be words of life rather than words of death. They will begin to move your life in the direction you want it to go. They will open doors of opportunity and deepen important relationships. The tremendous creative force your words carry can be wielded most powerfully when you first use it to engage with the Giver in the most important conversations you'll ever have.

Chapter 4

# GO AHEAD—TALK
# TO YOURSELF

*Watch your thoughts; they become words.*

Frank Outlaw

*May the words of my mouth and the meditation of my heart*
*be pleasing to you, O LORD, my rock and my redeemer.*

King David (Ps. 19:14)

Go to any metropolitan city in the world—and even some not so metropolitan—and you will inevitably see someone walking down the street talking to himself. Your tendency, like mine, is probably to pity him for being disturbed as you watch his one-sided conversation out of the corner of your eye. The irony is that you and I carry on conversations with ourselves all the time too—just not usually out loud. Sometimes we may not even realize we are doing it. But whether we're aware of it or not, you and I talk to ourselves all day, every day, through the thoughts we allow to consume our minds.

Even if you have never keyed into them, your conscious and subconscious thoughts are your constant companions. They drive and form your every waking moment. How you choose to direct your thoughts will ultimately define your life. James Allen wrote in the classic work on this topic, *As a Man Thinketh,*

Man is made or unmade by himself; in the armory of thought he forges the weapons by which he destroys himself; he also fashions the tools with which he builds for himself heavenly mansions of joy and strength and peace. By the right choice and true application of thought, man ascends to the Divine Perfection; by the abuse and wrong application of thought, he descends below the level of the beast. Between these two extremes are all the grades of character, and man is their maker and master.[1]

You are made or unmade by your thoughts. Day after day, month after month, year after year, they create every condition of your life, so much so that situations and circumstances you perceive as happening *to* you are usually happening *because of* you, in one way or another. That's a tough pill to swallow, isn't it? No matter what the current state of your life is, your cumulative thoughts have landed you there. And every day they either keep you where you are, pull you backward, or propel you into a better future.

What you see and what you hear depends a great deal on where you are standing. It also depends on what sort of person you are.

C. S. Lewis

The good news is that you get to choose whether what goes on in your head works for you or against you. You have the capacity to maximize the thoughts that are beneficial to your faith, your success, your relationships, your health, and every other area of your life, and to disregard those that would try to keep you from attaining the full measure of what God has for you. This powerful reality has been co-opted and skewed in the past by nonbiblical thinkers, but in its original form, it is God's idea. He not only gives us the power to control our thoughts and to use them to cooperate with his plan for us, but he also tells us to do just that.

We've already discussed how words have creation power. This power begins with the words that fill your mind. Your dominating thoughts create your reality. How? First, they fashion your beliefs. Valid or not, those beliefs shape your attitudes about yourself and the world around you. Your attitudes create your feelings, and your feelings drive the actions you take in every area of your life.[2] The way you see yourself and the world around you is an outgrowth of what goes on in your mind. Everything you choose to do or not do, say or not say starts with the seed of thought. As such, getting a handle on the words no one hears but you is nonnegotiable when it comes to creating the life you are meant to live.

## GROWING THE GOOD

Have you ever taken the idea of sowing and reaping to heart? I'm sure you've heard it said, "You will reap what you sow." Yes, it's a farming principle—your harvest will be the result of the type and quality of the seeds you plant—but only on the surface. The truth of sowing and reaping applies to every area of life. When it comes to the words that fill your mind, this principle can make or break you. Writing to the church in Galatia, Paul described its unavoidability:

> Don't be misled: *No one makes a fool of God. What a person plants, he will harvest.* The person who plants selfishness, ignoring the needs of others—ignoring God!—harvests a crop of weeds. All he'll have to show for his life is weeds! But the one who plants in response to God, letting God's Spirit do the growth work in him, harvests a crop of real life, eternal life. (Gal. 6:7–8 MSG)

Not only does the soil have to be healthy, but you also have to plant the right thing in that soil. Every one of your thoughts is a seed that will, eventually, reap a harvest. What kind of harvest that is will be determined by what kind of seeds you sow. The very life you live is the bounty of your thoughts—its makeup completely determined by what you choose to plant. Along these lines, James Allen wrote,

> Man's mind may be likened to a garden, which may be intelligently cultivated or allowed to run wild; but whether cultivated or neglected, it must, and will, *bring forth.* If no useful seeds are put into it, then an abundance of useless weed-seeds will *fall* therein, and will continue to produce their kind.

Just as a gardener cultivates his plot, keeping it free from weeds, and growing the flowers and fruits which he requires, so may a man tend the garden of his mind, weeding out all the wrong, useless, and impure thoughts, and cultivating toward perfection the flowers and fruits of right, useful, and pure thoughts. By pursuing this process, a man sooner or later discovers that he is the master-gardener of his soul, the director of his life. He also reveals, within himself, the laws of thought, and understands, with ever-increasing accuracy, how the thought-forces and mind elements operate in the shaping of his character, circumstances, and destiny.[3]

Your thoughts act as instructions to your brain; as soon as they come through, your brain goes to work to turn them into reality. Or in keeping with the analogy, when you plant seeds of thought—no matter what kind of seeds they are—your brain gets busy producing a corresponding crop. Your subconscious mind can't differentiate between useful seeds and weed-seeds, or between what's true and beneficial to you and what's not. It simply keys into the thoughts running around in your head, takes them at face value, and begins the process of growing them. That being the case, you and I need to step back and think about what we are saying to ourselves in our ongoing internal conversations and start using words that will reap a harvest of peace, joy, and fulfillment rather than those that choke out the life we want.

Watch your thoughts; they become words.

Watch your words; they become actions.

Watch your actions; they become habits.

Watch your habits; they become character.

Watch your character, for it becomes your destiny.

                                                    Anonymous

There are three main areas of life where your thoughts produce an obvious, measurable harvest: your personal accomplishments, your relationships, and your health. Let's look at how each of these areas is inextricably tied to what you say when you talk to yourself.

## 1. PERSONAL ACHIEVEMENT

Every accomplishment in your life—whether it's how well you do in school, what level you ascend to in your professional life, or how you manage your household—is directly linked to how you feel about yourself, to whether or not you think you are capable and worthy of living life at the highest level. And what defines your evaluation of your own capabilities and worth? What you say about yourself when you talk to yourself. Or as author Stephen Covey likes to put it, the "mental script" from which you operate.[4]

Your mental script has been developing since the day you were born. It began with what your parents said to you. If your parents, intentionally or otherwise, made comments that led you to believe you weren't smart enough, cute enough, or good enough, those hurtful words and the emotions that accompany them started setting the foundation for how you see yourself. Along the way, friends, teachers, and personal experiences have built on that foundation, shaping how you think about yourself and thereby shaping what you think you can do and be in this world. After all, what you believe about yourself determines how you feel about yourself; how you feel about yourself dictates your daily actions; and your daily actions added up over time determine your level of accomplishment in the areas of life that are important to you.

When you and I wake up to this reality, we can begin to filter the contents of our mental script through the sieve of truth, keeping what's beneficial and discarding what's not—a process that's crucial to creating a mental atmosphere that will allow us to operate at the full potential God has put in us. If we don't, we will end up living out our stories based on the incomplete and often inaccurate scripts that have been handed to us by others. Covey wrote,

> These scripts come from people, not principles. And they rise out of our deep vulnerabilities, our deep dependency on others and our needs for acceptance and love, for belonging, for a sense of importance, for a feeling that we matter.
>
> Whether we are aware of it or not, whether we are in control of it or not, there is a first creation to every part of our lives. We are either the second creation of our own proactive design, or we are the second creation of other people's agenda, of circumstances or of past habits.[5]

Becoming "the second creation of our own proactive design" requires that we become aware of how we think about our value, our abilities, our dreams, and our goals, getting rid of misinformation that isn't helping us live as the people we know we can be and focusing instead on our true identities—identities that start to become clear when we choose to view ourselves through the lens of scriptural truth. Consider this handful of the many verses that speak to who we really are:

> For we are God's masterpiece. He has created us anew in Christ Jesus, so we can do the good things he planned for us long ago. (Eph. 2:10)

> God created human beings in his own image. In the image of God he created them. (Gen. 1:27)

> For you created my inmost being; you knit me together in my mother's womb. I praise you because I am fearfully and wonderfully made. (Ps. 139:13–14 NIV)

> See how very much our Father loves us, for he calls us his children, and that is what we are! (1 John 3:1)

> Do you not know that you are the temple of God and that the Spirit of God dwells in you? (1 Cor. 3:16 NKJV)

"For I know the plans I have for you," says the
LORD. "They are plans for good and not for disaster,
to give you a future and a hope." (Jer. 29:11)

When you think negatively about yourself, you are putting
down God. You are his child, created in his image. He has knit you
together with meticulous care, filled you with potential, and given
you everything you need to accomplish the purposes he has for you.
Why, then, would you choose to spend precious time operating from
a place of self-doubt and pessimism that will do nothing but undermine the level of your life?

You get to decide what mental script you allow to direct your
thoughts and dictate your days—the script that has come to you
from well-intentioned but often misguided people speaking out of
their own poor scripts, *or* a script based on the true identity God has
given you. Choose wisely; your decision will determine the directives
your subconscious mind receives and thereby control the direction
and quality of your life.

## 2. RELATIONSHIPS

Your thought life also manifests itself in the quality of your relationships with others. That's because how you think and feel about
yourself dictates how you interact with people. For example, if you
see yourself as shy or socially awkward, that belief will lead you to
avoid social situations and lose out on the relationships you may find
through them. If you avoid connecting with other people because
you're afraid you won't be liked or that you'll get hurt, you are crippling your life based on fear—fear that's counter to who you were

created to be and perpetuated by the words you allow to run around in your head. Do you ever find yourself thinking things like the following?

> *I always say the wrong thing when I talk to her.*
> *I don't get along well with other people.*
> *Relationships are hard for me.*
> *I'm so uncomfortable in social settings.*

Phrases like these put you on the path to relational dissatisfaction. They become self-fulfilling prophecies. You may very well say the wrong thing when you talk to people, but if you do, it's because you expect to; you are living by the mental script that mandates it. If you have told yourself that you're not good at relating to other people or maintaining long-term relationships, your subconscious is working to fulfill those thought patterns. If it hears you say, *Oh, I always feel so awkward in large groups of people*, then guess what? You'll dread the next social gathering you're invited to and then not enjoy it once you're there.

On the other hand, if you shift what you say when you talk to yourself and instead think things like, *I love being with and talking with the people in my life. I'm thankful that I am able to connect with others and express myself clearly* or *I'm open to relationships. I'm comfortable being myself and accepting others for who they are*, then the way you engage with other people will change. Your subconscious will follow the new instructions and turn them into reality just as easily as it followed the old. With some time and repetition, it really is that simple.

You can sabotage your relational life not only by thinking the wrong thing about yourself but also by dwelling on the wrong thoughts when it comes to other people. For example, do you ever think things like the following?

> *My mother and I have so many issues; I don't think*
> *we'll ever work through them.*
> *My spouse and I just don't get along like we used to.*
> *My friends are so annoying. Why do I even spend time*
> *with them?*

I'm not saying you need to lie to yourself; thoughts like these may have truth to them. You and your mother may have complicated, deep-seated issues. But if you want to build your relationship with her, you can't let those issues dominate your thinking. Instead, make a decision to focus on the good in your relationship. Think on what you love about her. Talk to yourself about those things. Not only will an intentionally renewed focus change the way you see her, but it will also change the way you talk to her. After all, as we've established, your words are a direct result of what's going on inside. Over time, your relationship will be transformed for the better because you made a choice to direct your thoughts in a beneficial way rather than letting them carry you down the path to perpetuated problems.

> The most influential person who will talk to you all day is you, so you should be very careful about what you say to you!
>
> Zig Ziglar

The same holds true for your spouse, your children, your friends, and your coworkers. You will see what you are looking for. If you constantly think about the problems in your relationships or the shortcomings of the people around you, you will only see those problems and shortcomings as you interact with them. If you focus instead on the good in the people in your life, you will start to see that good manifest itself. This simple tweak in the words you allow to fill your head will shift your entire perspective, strengthening and growing even your most tenuous relationships.

## 3. HEALTH

How do you feel today? Are you tired? Are you sick? Maybe you're feeling healthy, happy, and on top of the world. Here's something that may surprise you: how you feel has almost everything to do with how you *think* you feel. If you wake up in the morning thinking about how tired you are and wishing you could just pull the covers over your head and stay put, then you will start the day feeling sluggish. Your body will respond to the directive of your thoughts by dragging through the morning, sans energy. Your entire day may play out at a subpar level because of the mental atmosphere you created for yourself before you even got out of bed.

On the other hand, if you wake up choosing to be grateful for another morning, focusing on how healthy you are and on the promise the day holds, your body will again respond accordingly. You'll move through your day with more energy and joy. You'll feel better, look better, and have more to offer those around you—and all because of what you chose to say to yourself when the alarm went off.

Your thoughts—the words of your mind—do not exist in a vacuum; they have creative power, just like the words that come out of your mouth do. What goes on in your head creates chemical realities within your body. Different thoughts and their accompanying emotions cause neurons to fire in your brain, setting off correlating physical reactions. This isn't new information. King Solomon wrote about it thousands of years ago: "A cheerful heart is good medicine, but a broken spirit saps a person's strength" (Prov. 17:22).

Dr. Norman Vincent Peale went a step further:

> The longer I live the more I am convinced that neither age nor circumstance needs to deprive us of energy and vitality. We are at last awakening to the close relationship between religion and health. We are beginning to comprehend a basic truth hitherto neglected, that our physical condition is determined very largely by our emotional condition, and our emotional life is profoundly regulated by our thought life.
>
> All through its pages, the Bible talks about vitality and force and life. The supreme over-all word of the Bible is life, and life means vitality—to be filled with energy.[6]

Science backs up both King Solomon's and Norman Vincent Peale's assertions. The stress that comes along with wrong thinking (and the resulting negative feelings and bad attitudes) raises blood pressure and releases the hormone cortisol into your system. When cortisol levels remain high over a period of time, they can lead to anxiety, weight gain, digestive problems, heart disease, and even cancer. Choosing to let those thoughts and accompanying emotions go in favor of more positive ones automatically improves your body's state of being, leading to better health and more vitality. Don't underestimate the power you have to put yourself on a healthier path simply by filling your head with the right thoughts.

## THINKING ABOUT THOUGHTS

Since the level of our lives is so directly tied to the quality of our internal dialogue, we must do what we can to shape that dialogue for our best interests. It's not enough just to understand the power of our thoughts or to know we need to change. We have to take specific action. Thankfully, there are three practical steps you and I can take to help us adopt consistently better thinking.

### 1. LISTEN TO YOUR INTERNAL DIALOGUE.

The first step to creating a healthier thought life doesn't require you to do anything but listen. A few chapters ago, I asked you to begin listening to what you say to other people on a daily basis. In the same way, you have to become aware of the script that's constantly running in your own head. When you talk to yourself, listen.

One of the main things that separates us from animals is our ability to think about our thought life—to note an individual thought passing through our minds, analyze it for its truth and worth, and then act on it accordingly. God gave us that unique ability when he made us in his image. But so often we let our thoughts run on autopilot. They are just there, and we don't give them much consideration. Or worse, we forget that we are the masters of our own thoughts and let them have their way with us. As you begin to tune in to your own mental environment, keep these basic truths about thoughts in mind:

- You can't always control the thoughts that pop into your head, but you can control what you do with them.
- Thoughts only have as much power as you give them. The more you dwell on a certain thought, the more powerful it will become.
- It's not a sin to have a wrong, negative, or tempting thought pass through your mind—if you let it pass right on through. The sin comes when you choose to indulge that thought, either by dwelling on it or acting on it.

Becoming aware of what's going on in your head is key to changing it for the better—but it's just the first step. Next, you have to take some directed action in response to what you hear.

## 2. TAKE EVERY THOUGHT CAPTIVE.

When God moves into the driver's seat of your heart, he begins to change you from the inside out—but you have to cooperate with what he's doing by taking an active role in directing your mind accordingly. As God begins to fill you with more peace, love, and joy, the effects of those gifts will be thwarted if you refuse to let them take root and influence your thoughts. It's up to you to resist habitual thought patterns and instead match your brain to the new thing God is doing in your spirit. How? By taking two steps Paul outlined in his letters to early Christian believers.

The first step is to take every thought captive: "Take captive every thought to make it obedient to Christ" (2 Cor. 10:5 NIV). This starts with listening to the thoughts in your head, but it goes further. You have to evaluate your thoughts, trapping and disposing of the ones that don't line up with God's truth.

Second, Paul says to "fix your thoughts on what is true, and honorable, and right, and pure, and lovely, and admirable. Think about things that are excellent and worthy of praise" (Phil. 4:8). In other words, be proactive in choosing how you focus your thoughts. When you capture and get rid of thoughts that are not in line with what God is working in your heart and then follow that up by shifting your attention to things that are true, right, and excellent, you will begin to see yourself and the world around you differently. Your self-image will improve; your relationships will become stronger; your body will be healthier. And that's all before words even begin coming out of your mouth.

There's one more key ingredient to making this shift— something that has to happen in the space between these two steps, causing them to work together to become a lifestyle rather than a short-term fix.

## 3. REPLACE OLD THINKING WITH NEW.

Psychologists tell us that you can't just get rid of a bad habit, including a negative thought pattern. You have to fill the vacated space with something new. Otherwise, your well-intentioned change won't last; you'll revert right back to comfortable habits and well-worn patterns. So as you begin eliminating thoughts that don't benefit you, you have to immediately replace those thoughts with new ones that do. As you ship out the internal dialogue that keeps you depressed, shy, anxious, tired, and worried, you have to immediately fill the space in your mind that those thoughts occupied with a corresponding positive internal dialogue. It's not enough to think about true, positive, pure, and excellent things in general. Connect them immediately to the vacated space of your captured thoughts. If you don't, those old thoughts will creep right back in.

One leading author on the topic describes this concept by viewing the mind as a mental apartment, furnished with the things you think about yourself and the world around you:

> [This furniture] is the old negative way of thinking which was handed down to us from our parents, our friends, our teachers…: they gave us the furniture which we have kept and which we use in our mental apartment.…
>
> Now let us say that I agree to come over to your home, this mental apartment, and help you get rid of all the old furniture.… We remove every piece, every dish, every rug, table, bed, sofa, and chair. We take out every old negative self-belief and store it away, safely out of sight.…
>
> After I leave you stand in the middle of your mental apartment.… You look around and think,

"This is great! I've gotten rid of all my old negative thinking...."

A little later that evening, after spending an hour or two with nothing but yourself and an empty apartment, what do you suppose you will do? You will go out into the garage where the old furniture is stored, and get a chair! A little later, you will make another trip to the garage and bring in a table....

One by one you will begin to bring your old trusted and time-worn negative thoughts back into your mental apartment! Why? Because when I helped you remove the old furniture I didn't give you any new furniture to replace it with—I didn't give you any positive new thoughts to replace the negative old thoughts.

When you decide to stop thinking negatively, and do not have an immediate, new positive vocabulary to replace the old, you will always return to the comfortable, old, negative self-talk of the past.[7]

Think back to the relationship examples above. When negative, defeating thoughts about your parents, your spouse, your children, or anyone else pop up, it's not enough to simply say to yourself, "Oh, I shouldn't think such a thing." Instead, you have to shift your focus toward something good, as we discussed. The most effective way to do that is to immediately replace the unproductive thought with a corresponding positive one. Out with the old, in with the new.

For example, if you find yourself thinking something uncon-structive such as, *I can't stand the way my children always second-guess me*, capture that thought, get rid of it, and then immediately fill the space with a better thought like, *My children are learning to question and discern the world around them for themselves. How can I produc-tively nurture that?* Don't just stop at getting rid of the unhealthy thought; instead, be intentional about putting something new in its place. Maybe you can see yourself in some of these other examples:

Old Thinking: *I feel so fat and unhealthy.*
Replacement: *My body is an amazing machine. I am healthy and well.*

Old Thinking: *I'm always tired.*
Replacement: *I feel great. I have so much energy today.*

Old Thinking: *I'm sick of my job.*
Replacement: *I'm thankful for my job and the income it creates.*

Old Thinking: *I'm not talented enough to do what I really want to do.*
Replacement: *I am blessed with incredible skills and abilities, and I use them to their full potential.*

You aren't being delusional or ignoring reality when you replace your negative thoughts with healthier, positive ones; you are simply choosing to see the other side of the coin. It has been there all along; you just haven't been looking at it. There's more than one way to think about every situation and event in your life. When you choose to see the positive, you are agreeing with God's perspective—you are agreeing with his view of you, your circumstances, and the people he has put around you. That alone will propel you toward a fuller, happier life. As Paul wrote,

> Don't copy the behavior and customs of this world, but *let God transform you into a new person by changing the way you think.* Then you will learn to know God's will for you, which is good and pleasing and perfect. (Rom. 12:2)

There it is. God is in the process of transforming you from the inside out, but he can't complete that work in you unless you let him, unless you cooperate with him by letting his thoughts become your thoughts. Do your part to step out of your old, ingrained thinking—the thinking that has left you feeling less than what you know you can be—and fill your mind instead with thoughts that can elevate you to the best, truest version of yourself, making you into the person ready to accept the abundant life God has in store (see John 10:10). Everything you are, everything you do, and everything you say begins in your mind. Cooperate with God in changing those words first, and your whole life will reflect the change.

Chapter 5

# THE LANGUAGE OF LOVE

*You never know when a moment and a few sincere*
*words can have an impact on a life.*

Zig Ziglar

*Love is patient and kind. Love is not jealous or boastful or*
*proud or rude. It does not demand its own way. It is not*
*irritable, and it keeps no record of being wronged.*

Paul (1 Cor. 13:4–5)

Relationship problems are, by and large, communication problems. No healthy relationship can exist in a space where there isn't healthy communication—but plenty of people try to force them to. You've known these people; maybe you have been one yourself. They are the ones who trudge on in a state of discontent long after thoughtful words have gone by the wayside. They continue to go through the motions of relationship, subsisting on the fumes of an earlier day when their connection was filled with clear, loving communication. But the way they have used or failed to use words over a period of time has landed them in a painful situation. The people in these relationships usually fall into one of two predictable categories: either they have nothing to say to each other, or everything they say is filled with disdain. Can you relate?

The quality of every relationship in your life will rise or fall based on the quality of the communication within that relationship. And since relationships are the building blocks of life itself, the level of your overall success and happiness will follow suit. Given this reality, learning to use words that foster healthy, growing communication with the people closest to you isn't just a good idea; it's integral to your well-being and theirs.

When the words in a relationship run dry or turn negative, the answer isn't to slog along unhappily. The answer isn't to throw the relationship away and set out in search of a new one that will theoretically make you happier. The answer is to go back to square one and reestablish—or establish for the first time—healthy communication. The kind of life-giving communication your relationships are thirsty for develops when you intentionally choose to do three things that come together to form the essential precept for using your words well with others:

> *Communicate:* At the most basic level, you have to talk to the people in your life. If you don't make the effort to communicate, there will be no relationship left to invest in.

> *Communicate Clearly:* As you communicate, keep clarity in mind. So many relationship problems happen not because people aren't talking, but because they are speaking two different languages. You have to be intentional about what you say and how you say it.

*Communicate Clearly with Love:* Finally, bathe that clear communication in love. You can communicate words of life just as clearly and easily as you can communicate words of death. If you want to have relationships that bring joy and confidence to you and the people closest to you, make sure every communication you have is filled with love.

Think of the three separate elements of communicating clearly with love as stepping stones that build on each other, creating the pathway to healthier relationships. When you embrace them, your relationships will move into a new realm. Let's dig into some specifics on how you can communicate clearly with love in two of the most foundational relationships in your life—in your marriage and with your kids.

## COMMUNICATE CLEARLY WITH LOVE—MARRIAGE

### *COMMUNICATE*

One afternoon many years ago, when my wife and I were just dating, we were having lunch at a small café in Boston. We were in our twenties and madly in love. Our words flowed freely. Shortly after we sat down, an older couple took the table right next to us. They ordered their lunch and then sat there across from each other in silence. When the waiter brought their food, they ate without saying a word, paid the bill, and left. All in all, the two probably didn't say more than five words to each other the whole time they were in the café. Their silence didn't seem like the comfortable result of many years together either; it seemed more like unhappy resignation. As soon as they were out the door, we couldn't help but comment on how strange it seemed to us that a couple could have absolutely nothing to say to each other—yet that scenario is much more common than we ever would have imagined at the time.

Somewhere along the way, this couple—like so many others—let their words dry up. It probably happened as a series of small concessions over the years. As life got busy with opposite work schedules and kids vying for attention, they probably stopped taking the time to tell each other the details about what was going on at the office or what the day was like at home. They probably stopped talking about their goals, their expectations, and their fears. Many couples do. In fact, the average married couple only spends four minutes per day alone together.[1] Over a week, that adds up to a whopping twenty-eight minutes. No intimate relationship can thrive on twenty-eight minutes of conversation per week. Our silent lunch mates likely fell into that twenty-eight-minute trap, let the lack of words between them morph into emotional distance, then woke up one day to find that there were no words to be found at all.

How can you make sure that this scenario doesn't become a reality in your own marriage? By being proactive about keeping the conversation of life alive. Start by carving out time for true communication. Not only do most couples only spend twenty-eight minutes per week talking, but when they do talk, that talk isn't life-giving in nature. Most of those minutes happen in the morning when the couple are rushed or in the evening when they're tired. During those moments, real conversation takes the backseat to who has to be where, when and what bills have to be paid from which account, and what day the in-laws are getting to town. You know the drill. It's impossible for intimacy to happen in that space. For intimacy to have a chance to thrive, it needs its own place to live; it needs both time and deep, meaningful words to nurture it.

Get practical about keeping the words in your relationship—and thereby your relationship—alive. Make a commitment to spend time together alone, talking about more than logistics, talking the way you used to talk when you shared everything with each other. Here are two practical ways to keep your line of communication open and clear:

**1. Schedule a regular date night.** Sit down with your calendars, and schedule some togetherness. Planning a date with your spouse like you plan a meeting may seem strange at first, but think of it this way—you are setting aside a space for real communication to happen. You are planning a time to get back to intentionally using your words in a way that stokes the fire of your love for each other. A regularly scheduled evening of one-on-one time with your spouse is one of the greatest gifts you can give each other, not to mention one of the surest ways to keep your relationship healthy.

Given your current situation, you may only be able to schedule a date night once a month. If you can, I highly recommend making it once a week. Whatever you decide you can do, put those nights on your calendar, and protect them. Look forward to them, and don't let anything else get in the way of them happening. Don't let work issues, last-minute school projects, sheer tiredness, or anything else encroach on them.

If you want to, you can make all kinds of excuses to let date night slip through the cracks. Maybe you think you can't afford it or you don't have anyone who could watch the kids. These and other little lies like them keep you and your spouse on the path of least resistance—a path that ultimately leads to the death of what's most important. Date nights don't have to be expensive. Every once in a while, you may want to do something special that costs more money—maybe for an anniversary or a birthday—but there are lots of ways to have romantic dates on a regular basis without stretching yourself financially. You could make a picnic and take it to a local park. Talk about what's happening in your lives and family while you eat your packed sandwiches. Or stay home, order a pizza, and linger over it. As far as the kids go, try trading date nights with another couple. Watch their kids so they can go out (or stay in) for an evening and then vice versa. Be creative. Don't let convenient excuses kill the covenant you made on the day you said "I do."

**2. Repeat your wedding vows.** When you stood at the altar, you used your words to enter into a covenant with your spouse and with God. You probably said something along the lines of this:

> I take you to be my wife/husband, to have and to
> hold from this day forward, for better or for worse,
> for richer, for poorer, in sickness and in health, to
> love and to cherish, until death do us part.

Talk about powerful words. Those marriage vows catapulted you into the deepest commitment two people can make to one another. Still, most people don't think much about the words from their wedding ceremony after they've been pronounced husband and wife. It's not that they aren't committed; it's just that life happens, and they simply don't take the time to revisit the specifics of what they promised.

One of the best ways to keep your relationship fresh and strong is to remind yourselves of the words that came out of your mouths on the day you became one. Your anniversary is a great time to revisit your vows. Why not make a commitment to repeat them to each other every year over your anniversary dinner? Take the opportunity to remind yourselves of the powerful union you spoke into being. Then make a fresh commitment to use your everyday words in a way that will support and continually breathe life into your relationship.

## COMMUNICATE CLEARLY

"Irreconcilable differences" is the number one reason divorcing couples cite for the deterioration of their marriages. But when those couples first walked to the altar, their differences were not so irreconcilable at all. In fact, their differences were probably what drew them to each other. I would bet that they used to sit up late at night talking about how they saw the world, how they envisioned their future, what dreams and goals they wanted to accomplish. But down the road, close to 60 percent of them are bolting for a lawyer's office, most claiming they just can't get along with this other person they thought they loved. What happened?

The term *irreconcilable differences* is code for "we don't know how to or aren't willing to communicate clearly." Paul Tournier, a Swiss psychiatrist who has written extensively on marriage, contends,

[Irreconcilable differences] is a myth invented by jurists short of arguments in order to plead for

divorce. It is likewise a common excuse people use
in order to hide their own failings. I simply do not
believe it exists. There are no emotional incompatibilities. There are misunderstandings and mistakes,
however, which can be corrected where there is a
willingness to do so. [2]

The entire idea of irreconcilable differences is built on the illu-
sion of incompatibility that has taken hold in our culture. Claiming
incompatibility is like throwing down the *get-out-of-jail-free* card. It
is nothing more than an excuse to end a relationship that doesn't feel
good anymore—usually because the parties involved haven't done
the work to keep it alive and thriving. Dr. Paul Popenoe, the late
director of the American Institute of Family Relations, once wrote
this about incompatibility:

> It would be hard to find a word that is so often
> used so unscientifically. Almost any two people are
> compatible if they try to be so.[3]

The problem is that when the ground starts to get shaky under-
foot, most people—the same ones who were once so in love that
they committed their futures to each other—stop trying. Instead,
they begin focusing their attention on and talking about all the
ways they are not well matched. Before you know it, their words
have strengthened those apparent incompatibilities and turned
them into reality. As a result, the no-longer-happy couple is headed
to court with an *irreconcilable differences* plea.

If you have ever seen a seedling of this phenomenon taking root in your relationship, be intentional about not allowing it to grow. If you'll make a concerted effort to communicate clearly with your partner, you can get back to appreciating the differences that first drew you together and continue building on the good in your relationship as it exists now. Start by focusing on what you do have in common and by identifying the kind of words—and thereby the kind of atmosphere—you want your relationship to be filled with.

## Clarify commonalities.

The biggest reason you and your spouse have communication problems is that you expect your spouse to think like you do. When that doesn't happen, you think there's a problem—and there is: The problem is your unwillingness to humble yourself and work to see things from your spouse's perspective. The smoke-and-mirrors claim of incompatibility simply masks stubbornness. Getting years into a relationship and then saying "We're too different to make it work" is just another way of saying "We're not willing to change; we're not willing to find the path to compromise."

The first step in moving back toward compatibility is to start reminding yourself of the time when you loved each other's differences, even as you begin creating some new commonalities between you. Identify some things you would enjoy doing together. Use part of the time you have during your date nights to make a list of projects you could take on or activities you could engage in. Reminisce about the fun you've had in the past, and talk about new experiences you'd like to have. If you don't, your marriage is going to go stale. Your words will flow less freely, your connection will weaken, and you'll find yourself in a difficult (or even more difficult) relationship.

### Identify acceptable and unacceptable words.

Defining what words are acceptable and unacceptable in your relationship will save you a world of hurt when things get hard. Not only will it help you fight fair during a disagreement, but it will also help you eliminate entire conversations that would do nothing but take you down the wrong path.

Start by eliminating all idle threats. Specifically, I suggest removing the word *divorce* from your vocabulary. When things get difficult, leveling a threat of divorce does nothing but make a bad situation even worse. Not to mention, it plants a destructive seed in both of your minds and dashes confidence in the security of your relationship. But if divorce isn't an option, then all of your energy—both conscious and subconscious—can go toward working out a solution to the problems you are facing. No matter how difficult the moment may seem, God always wants to do great things in your marriage. But you have to cooperate with him by choosing to avoid words that undermine your relationship and focusing on words that strengthen it.

## COMMUNICATE CLEARLY WITH LOVE

No marriage can exist in perpetual harmony. There will be misunderstandings and conflict. That's okay. In fact, when two people agree on everything, one of them isn't necessary. As Sir Alan Patrick Herbert said,

> The conception of two people living together for twenty-five years without having a cross word suggests a lack of spirit only to be admired in sheep.

Since arguments are inevitable, the key is to cover them—and all communication within your marriage—with love.

## Surrender the right to be right.

My wife, Kelley, and I tend to argue over the smallest things. Can you relate? The majority of our fights aren't over big decisions or future hopes and dreams, but over mundane nothingness. Over the years, I've learned that when it comes to arguing over the small stuff, you have a choice: you can choose to be right, or you can choose to be happy. Consider what Paul's mentee, Timothy, wrote:

> Remind everyone about these things, and command them in God's presence to stop fighting over words. Such arguments are useless, and they can ruin those who hear them.... Again I say, don't get involved in foolish, ignorant arguments that only start fights. (2 Tim. 2:14, 23)

Humility is the underlying issue when it comes to surrendering your right to be right. When you are humble, you don't feel the need to come out on top all the time. You don't have to win every battle. You are able to admit when you are wrong. Next time you feel your temper rising over something relatively insignificant, just pause and ask yourself if that thing is worth a fight, if it's worth ruining your day. If not, be humble enough to be the one who bows out of the scuffle. Surrender your right to prove that you are in the right. Being able to do that actually makes you the winner.

### Choose kindness.

Be considerate of your spouse. Intentionally use words that are full of love. Most couples are overflowing with kindness and consideration toward one another early on in their courtship and in the first few years of marriage, but with time and familiarity, that kindness often gets traded in for less beneficial communication. Take a look at this little ditty that underscores the slide:

> *Two young lovers walked down the street.*
> *She tripped and he worried, "Be careful, sweet."*
> *Now, married, they walk down the exact same street,*
> *But when she trips, he says, "Pick up your feet!"*

Not only does the quality of our words seem to deteriorate over the years, but we are also prone to save our harshest words for the people we care about the most. A recent University of Denver study examined the speech habits of couples during their first and second decades of marriage. The results were interesting but not at all surprising. Among couples that ended up staying together and having successful marriages, less than 5 percent of the comments they made to one another were negative. But among the couples that later split up, twice as many of their comments—around 10 percent—were negative, usually in the form of biting personal remarks or put-downs.

> Think twice before you speak, because your words and influence will plant the seed of either success or failure in the mind of another.
>
> Napoleon Hill

Over the second decade of marriage, the couples that ultimately divorced had worked their way up to flinging five times as many cruel and belittling comments at each other as the couples that stayed happily married. The study concluded that harsh words and insults in a marriage act as cancerous cells that, if left unchecked, erode the relationship over time.[4] After a while, unremitting negativity takes control, and the couple can't get through a day without a major blowup. Arguing and inflicting wounds on one another becomes the norm, wearing both parties down to the point of sheer exhaustion.

Since word choice is the single most reliable indicator of whether a marriage is going to succeed or fail, make an intentional decision to avoid the trap of speaking to your spouse thoughtlessly. Choose kind words instead. Stop pointing out everything he or she does wrong. Stop nitpicking. That's not your role anyway. Your job is to love and to make every effort to help your spouse fulfill his or her God-given potential.

The words that accompany an attitude of kindness also continually reinforce it. For example, when you speak kind words to your spouse, he or she is more likely to reciprocate the effort. Over a period of time, that simple step will lead to more love between you. Here are two of the best, most effective ways you can use kind words to bolster the love in your relationship:

**1. Praise your spouse in public.** When you are around friends and family members, speak well of your spouse. Make a point of complimenting him or her. Tell a story about something great he did. There's not much that will make your spouse swell with love and affection for you more than hearing words of affirmation spoken in the presence of others. Conversely, there's no better way to undermine a relationship than to speak negatively to or about your spouse in front of other people.

**2. Avoid sarcasm and harsh words masked as jokes.** Inappropriate joking (and its sister, sarcasm) is one of the most common mistakes I see men make with their wives. Until they learn better, most men think they can josh around with their wife in the same way they do with their buddies; this kind of joking usually consists of poking fun and trash-talking. But most women don't respond well to that kind of communication, even when they know it's in jest. Instead of trying to prove that there's no harm in talking that way, be mindful of how your spouse wants to be communicated with, and humble yourself to honor that. As you both take this step and become mutually respectful of each other's sensitivities, your communication and your love will become deeper than you knew was possible.

In the greatest chapter on love in the entire Bible, the apostle Paul wrote,

> Love is patient and kind. Love is not jealous or boastful or proud or rude. It does not demand its own way. It is not irritable, and it keeps no record of being wronged. It does not rejoice about injustice but rejoices whenever the truth wins out. Love never

gives up, never loses faith, is always hopeful, and
endures through every circumstance. (1 Cor. 13:4–7)

Those are wise words for us to live by in our love relationships. If
we can learn to give away love that is patient and kind, not jealous,
proud, boastful, rude, or irritable; if we can love in a way that causes
us to never keep a record of wrongs (that's a big one, isn't it?); if we
can learn to walk in love that never loses faith and is always hopeful;
if we can learn to live a love that endures through every circumstance,
then we will have cultivated a love that will allow our marriages to
thrive at the highest level.

## COMMUNICATE CLEARLY WITH LOVE—CHILDREN

### COMMUNICATE

I'm convinced that the holy grail of parenting rests in how well you
communicate with your children. The power of parent-child communication begins with you being intentional about developing a
clear, flowing line of communication with your children from an
early age. I have to credit my mom with being a pro at this. Growing
up, I used to tell her everything. From the time I could speak, she
used her words to encourage mine. Over the years, she cultivated an
open line of communication with me that not only created a strong
relationship between us but also helped me make wise decisions as I
navigated the path to adulthood.

For example, knowing that I would be telling my mom about
what happened at a party I went to or at a friend's house when the
parents weren't there—not because I was forced to tell her or because

I felt obligated to, but just because that's the kind of relationship that had always existed between us—kept me behaving in a way that I wouldn't be ashamed to talk about. As part of our rapport, she had always clearly expressed her confidence that I would make wise decisions (another key), so I did my best to live up to that expectation. Because of the candidness and trust between us, I didn't want to lie or hide anything from her, so I carried myself through dicey teenage situations in a way that I knew I could talk about without embarrassment—and if I stumbled, I knew I could tell her that, too. She understood that I wasn't perfect and was quick to show me grace when I needed it.

What my mother—and other wise parents like her—understood was that the words that flow between a parent and a child are the air that gives life to the relationship. How much time and effort you invest in communicating well with your children will pay huge dividends in the relationship you have with them as they move into adulthood. Not only will your level of communication with them determine the quality of your connection later, but it will also go a long way toward defining the course of their lives.

## Listen to your kids.

If you want your children to talk openly with you as they grow into teenagers and young adults, then you have to start actively listening to what they want to say from the time they first start speaking. As author Catherine Wallace wrote,

> Listen earnestly to anything your children want to
> tell you, no matter what. If you don't listen eagerly

to the little stuff when they are little, they won't tell
you the big stuff when they are big, because to them
all of it has always been big stuff.[5]

Children are surprisingly observant. They watch and internalize
every reaction you have to them. If they think you aren't interested in
what they are saying, they receive an internal message that something
else is more important to you than they are, that you don't really
care about their interests. That message—whether true or not—will
slowly undermine your best efforts at open communication.

As your children learn to use their words, engage them. Encourage
them to talk to you about anything and everything. Nothing is off-
limits. Decide to be interested in whatever they are interested in. If
you have a son or a daughter who is a science buff, but you know
nothing about science, you'd better start studying. When they talk
to you about their discoveries, be as excited as they are. As they get
older, keep them talking. Don't leave the conversation up to them.
Ask about what's going on in their lives, and actively listen to what
they say. No matter how busy you are, put the work aside, put your
phone down, look them in the eye, and listen—fully and earnestly.

## COMMUNICATE CLEARLY

As you know by now, you are picking sides in the battle between
life and death every time you open your mouth. Not only are you
directing your own life toward one side over the other, but you are
also taking other people along with you. Nowhere is this truer than
in your relationship with your children. The words you choose to say
to them—or to withhold from them—during their developmental

years will influence how they interact with the world throughout their lifetimes. As a parent, you have a great responsibility to communicate words that will help your children grow into healthy adults capable of achieving the full potential within them. Keeping that end goal in mind as you communicate with your children every day will help you choose words that clearly express life, worth, and positive value—in short, words that encourage.

## Speak words that encourage.

The word *encourage* literally means "to fill someone's life with courage." Children have not just a desire but a need to hear encouraging words from their parents. When they're young, the parental relationship is where they find the full sum of their identity and self-worth. They are looking to you to tell them they matter, to tell them they have something to offer the world. If they don't get the right kind of validation from you, they will eventually go looking for it elsewhere—which isn't what any concerned parent wants.

> A torn jacket is soon mended; but hard words bruise the heart of a child.
>
> Henry Wadsworth Longfellow

Your words have immense power to shape your children's destiny. What you say gives them the script for how they view themselves, which will largely determine their success in life's various arenas. Your words can either be used as tools to build them up or as weapons to tear them down; you get to choose. Do you want to be someone who speaks light and life to your kids, or do you want to be remembered for working in words that are dark, coarse, and dispiriting? Do you want to be their source of greatest encouragement or a hindrance to their efforts to live the best life possible?

In high school, the star running back on our school's football team and I were good friends. During our junior year, my friend felt like he was being called to more important pursuits than football and decided to leave the team. His father, with whom he had always had a fairly strong, if sometimes strained, relationship, didn't like the decision. In a heated discussion, my friend's father said to him, "You're just a quitter." Fast-forward twenty years. After hitting a major professional milestone, my friend and his father were sitting and talking. When his father offered congratulations for all that was going on in my friend's life, the first words that sprang from his lips were, "Not bad for a quitter, huh, Dad?" The father didn't even remember calling his son a quitter all those years ago, but the word had wounded my friend's heart. He'd been carrying it with him for over two decades. The words you and I speak to our children so flippantly carry enormous power in their hearts and minds.

Similarly, many parents think they are doing their children a favor by withholding praise. They're afraid they'll spoil their children if they speak affirmation to them. But that's a fallacy. While you shouldn't pour empty or overwrought praise on your kids, you should never neglect to affirm how important they are, how much they are loved, and how well they are doing. Your silence doesn't make them stronger; it inhibits their healthy development. In *The*

*Blessing: Giving the Gift of Unconditional Love and Acceptance,* authors John Trent and Gary Smalley wrote,

> For a child in search of the blessing, silence communicates mostly confusion. Children who are left to fill in the blanks when it comes to what their parents think about them will often fail the test when it comes to feeling valuable and secure. Spoken or written words at least give the child an indication that he or she is worthy of some attention....
>
> Good intentions aside, good *words*—spoken, written, and preferably both—are necessary to communicate genuine acceptance.[6]

Never withhold clear, loving encouragement from your children. Keep those lines of communication open, listen to what they have to say, clearly speak words of life and encouragement to them. And as you do those things, make sure you always communicate love by choosing your responses wisely.

## COMMUNICATE CLEARLY WITH LOVE

The moment you start responding to what your children have to say with indifference, negativity, or judgment, the lines of communication you've worked so hard to build will begin collapsing. Your children need to know that they can come to you with anything and that they won't be judged, talked down to, or made to feel like they are disappointing you. The impetus is on you to communicate with them clearly even in—especially in—difficult situations. The key is to choose your words wisely and to bathe those words in love.

## Choose your words wisely.

As you build open pathways of communication with your children, there will inevitably come a time when they will tell you something they've done or something they're struggling with that you don't like. At least, you should hope this time comes; if it doesn't, they're just hiding those things from you. Be careful of the words you choose when you are upset. They have the ability to damage not only your child's psyche but also the relationship between the two of you.

While you may be disappointed in a certain behavior, being disappointed in your child's behavior and being disappointed *in him* are two very different things. Choose words that reflect that reality. Make sure your child knows that just because he did something you don't like, that doesn't mean you love him any less. His actions don't dictate your level of love and commitment to him. This is where a lot of parents trip up. They fail to separate the behavior from the child and end up making the child feel like a disappointment.

Once you speak disappointment into a child's identity, you can't take it back. Not only does he feel a crack in his relationship with you, but your hurtful words also go to work, creating the reality you've spoken into motion. The "I'm a disappointment" seed takes root in the child's mind and begins to grow, negatively influencing his actions going forward. Of course, you should encourage your children to make the best choices, but you should be extremely careful about doing that in a way that doesn't express judgment over choices they've already made and the realities that exist because of those choices.

Some parents worry that showing unconditional love will give their child a free pass to do whatever he wants. Instead, it actually encourages him to act in a way worthy of that love. When healthy, this parent-child relationship perfectly mirrors the relationship that you and I have with God as we put our trust in him as our heavenly Father. We don't obey and do the right thing out of obligation but because his great love makes us want to do the things that will please him. When you and I mess up, God doesn't shame or chastise us; instead, he continues to show us deep, unwavering love as he gently prompts us back toward the best path (see John 8:4–11). People who incorrectly see God as a judge are much more likely to shut him out when they do something wrong, whereas people who understand his unconditional grace know that they can turn to him in any situation and that they will be met with overflowing love and forgiveness, which makes them want to act in a way more worthy of that love the next time. So it goes with our children.

Here's the simple fact: If your children feel judged by you, they will stop talking to you. If you create an environment where they feel like they can't be honest about who they really are and what they are struggling with, they will begin living the parts of their lives that they think would disappoint you under the radar. When that happens, your relationship with them and the direction of their lives will suffer the consequences. Instead of pushing them that way, keep encouraging them to talk. Keep listening well and choosing your responses thoughtfully. No matter what they tell you, show them love. Judgment and harsh words won't keep them heading in the right direction; your words of wisdom spoken from a heart of unconditional love will.

## COMMUNICATE. CLEARLY. WITH LOVE.

Communicating clearly with love is foundational to living the tongue-pierced life. You get to play a defining role in the quality of the relationships in your life through the words you speak. If your marriage isn't at its best, your words can turn it around for the better. If your relationship with your children isn't where you want it to be, some intentional tweaking in how you communicate can work wonders. Don't take that power for granted. Make the decision to communicate clearly with love in every important relationship in your life. Over time, you'll be amazed by what happens as a result.

*Chapter 6*

# DEVELOPING AN ATTITUDE OF GRATITUDE

*As we express our gratitude, we must never
forget that the highest appreciation
is not just to utter the words, but to live by them.*
John F. Kennedy

*Rejoice always, pray without ceasing, in everything give thanks;
for this is the will of God in Christ Jesus for you.*
Paul (1 Thess. 5:16–18 NKJV)

When my son started talking, *thank you* was one of the first phrases we taught him to say. I don't think that's unusual. After *mama, dada,* and a few other baby words, *thank you* is drilled into most children's heads early on. When they hand us a soggy cracker they've been gumming, we say, "Thank you." When someone gives them a gift or a compliment, we are quick to prompt, "What do you say?" to which they gurgle "Tank ouuu" or something to that effect, depending on their age. Even though they don't comprehend the significance of what they are saying, we make them say it anyway—and not simply because we place a high value on good manners. It's more than that. We understand the importance of expressing sincere gratitude to those who show us a kindness. Well, most of us do.

On that note, how do you feel when someone should say thank you but doesn't? Have you ever gone out of your way to do something nice for another person only to feel a little jilted when he or she doesn't say thanks? When you give a gift, you expect a thank-you note—or at least an email or phone call. When you pick up the bill at dinner, you expect your dining companions to show a little gratitude. Getting that gratitude isn't your goal when you take care of the check, give a gift, or do any other thoughtful thing, but still such courtesy shouldn't be neglected. When it is, you walk away feeling a little taken advantage of, right?

## MORE THAN MANNERS

While we teach our children to say thank you and try to remember to say thank you in our own lives, we often have to deal with the ripple effects of ingratitude—both others' and our own. This problem isn't anything new. Jesus faced the same thing in his day. One afternoon during his ministry, while he was on a journey from Galilee to Judea, Jesus passed through a place called Samaria. As he walked along the road, he saw ten lepers standing at a distance trying to get his attention. They were crying out, "Jesus, Master, have mercy on us!" (Luke 17:13).

We don't hear much about leprosy these days, but in Jesus's time it was serious business. Leprosy was considered not only extremely contagious but also incurable, which is why these ten lepers were standing apart from everyone else. When people were diagnosed with the disease, they were sent to a quarantined area, known as a leper colony, to live with other lepers. They lost their families and their livelihoods. They were destined to live in exclusion until they got an infection through their rotted skin and died. In short, leprosy was a death sentence that stole not only the victim's health but also his entire life.

Enter Jesus. When he heard the lepers calling to him, Jesus took one look in their direction and said, "Go show yourselves to the priests" (Luke 17:14). As the lepers began hobbling away, their disease suddenly disappeared. They were completely healed. Two minutes before, they had been destined to face the rest of their lives miserable and lonely, but now they would be able to return home to their families and go back to their jobs. They would be able to reenter their communities and reengage with their friends. What a miracle! You would think they would be clamoring over one another to thank Jesus and give glory to God for their healing, but Luke's account of the story reveals just the opposite:

> One of them, when he saw that he was healed, came back to Jesus, shouting, "Praise God!" He fell to the ground at Jesus' feet, thanking him for what he had done. This man was a Samaritan. Jesus asked, "Didn't I heal ten men? Where are the other nine? Has no one returned to give glory to God except this foreigner?" And Jesus said to the man, "Stand up and go. Your faith has healed you." (Luke 17:15–19)

Weren't the other nine lepers just as grateful for the miracle that had been done on their behalf as this one who returned to Jesus to say thanks? Where were they?

Jesus's encounter (or lack thereof) with this group of lepers reveals four truths about how we express gratitude in our own lives and how that gratitude (or lack thereof) ultimately shapes our every-day experiences.

## 1. GOD OFTEN GETS FORGOTTEN IN THE GOOD TIMES.

While you and I can easily see the glaring ingratitude of the lepers' response, we're often guilty of treating God the same way. We don't have leprosy, but most of us do suffer from a condition I call *gratitude deficiency*. Gratitude deficiency is characterized by a tendency to forget God when life is going well. If we're honest, our response to the good things that come our way probably looks more like the nine healed men who didn't come back to thank Jesus than the one who did.

While God is the source of every positive thing we experience (see James 1:17), a lot of times we take the credit ourselves, or we think we are just having a stroke of luck. Ironically, when things turn sour, we are quick with one of two responses: we either drop to our knees to beg for help, or we get angry with God for the hardship we're facing. Have you been there? Walking in a state of ungratefulness clouds our perception of the experiences in our lives and causes us to blame God for things that aren't his fault while neglecting to thank him for the good he's doing. That's a backward mind-set that can only hurt us over time.

## 2. GOD BLESSES THE GRATEFUL AND THE UNGRATEFUL.

Thanks to the concept of *common grace*, God's blessings are available to both those who show gratitude and those who don't. He loves every one of us, not because of what we do or how we treat him, but because we are his creation. Failing to thank him for what he does doesn't mean he's going to remove his blessings. Even though nine of the ten lepers didn't say thanks for the healing, they stayed well. Despite their attitude of ingratitude, they got to keep the blessing that had been given to them. In the same way, whether you live a life bent on having your own way or a life focused on God's purposes, you will receive some blessing. That said, when you choose to acknowledge God in your life and walk in step with him, you open yourself up to more of what he wants to do in, through, and for you. (Interested in learning more about *common grace*? Check out the list of resources on the subject at TonguePierced.com.)

## 3. GRATEFUL WORDS REFLECT GREATER FAITH.

Most people subscribe to one of two worldviews. The first contends that what happens in life happens by pure chance, that everything is accidental, and there's no design or purpose behind the events that make up our days. In this worldview, God is essentially removed from the picture, which makes ultimate gratitude unnecessary. There is no point in saying thank you for anything. After all, who would you even say thank you to? And why?

The other worldview is the biblical view that God is behind everything, that nothing happens by accident but instead is part of his divine order. This worldview holds that there is inherent purpose in every circumstance of your life and that God is constantly working the details together for your good and his glory. As Paul wrote,

> And we know that God causes everything to work
> together for the good of those who love God and

are called according to his purpose for them.
(Rom. 8:28)

When you choose to express your gratitude to God, you are acknowledging that you live by this worldview. You're exercising faith that God's ways are bigger than your own and that he is ultimately in control of every facet of your life. As a result, you open yourself up to seeing and receiving even more of God's goodness. You won't miss the things he does, because you'll be on the lookout for them. And each time he blesses you, your faith will grow even more.

## 4. GRATEFUL WORDS LEAD TO ADDITIONAL INTANGIBLE BLESSINGS.

When the one grateful leper came back to say thank you to Jesus, he received a blessing the other nine lepers didn't receive. Jesus's assertion, "Your faith has healed you" (Luke 17:19), refers not to the physical healing from leprosy but to an additional healing—a spiritual healing. In the same way, when you give God credit for what's happening in your life, he is going to bless you spiritually by drawing you closer to him. He will make you more aware of his day-to-day presence, and he will give you deeper glimpses into how he is working through the people and events around you.

One of the most common reasons people begin to feel distant from God is because they have slowly backed away from living a life of gratitude. As a result, their hearts have hardened. The failure to acknowledge what God is doing and to thank him for it is one of the quickest ways to throw up a roadblock in your relationship with him. But as you choose to walk with an attitude of gratitude and use your words to express thanks, the connection between you and God will stay strong, and he will be able to continue pouring his spiritual blessings into your life.

## ATTITUDE IS EVERYTHING

As with all words, *thank you* and other expressions of gratitude are key building blocks of the attitudes you and I walk around with. When we speak thankful words, even if we aren't necessarily feeling thankful in the moment, their creative power goes to work, fostering a more grateful attitude within us. That, in turn, will usher us into a more full and joyous life.

Harnessing the creative force of your words through directed action is the single best way to cultivate a mind-set that positively influences every aspect of your life. You can begin intentionally incorporating words of gratitude into everyday speech by taking some practical action steps based on the four truths above:

- Begin your day with gratefulness.
- Remove all complaints from your life.
- Be quick to say "Thank You."
- Learn to live every day in a state of present joy.

Let's dive into each one of these in more detail.

### *BEGIN YOUR DAY WITH GRATEFULNESS.*

Have you ever noticed that your mornings have a major impact on how your afternoon and evening hours unfold? If you get up when you are supposed to and have time to go through your morning routine without being rushed, that positive start generally sets you up for a good day. On the other hand, if you oversleep, don't have time for breakfast, don't have any time to spend with God, and rush out the door frazzled, that state of being is going to carry over into everything you do and every interaction you have for the rest of the day. Given this reality, choosing to take the time to focus on God with gratefulness first thing in the morning goes a long way toward keeping you in a grateful mind-set throughout the rest of the day.

To begin orienting yourself toward daily gratefulness, try starting a gratitude journal. Every morning, jot down five things you are grateful for. They may be specific things that happened in your life the day before, or they may be more general notions. On the mornings when you aren't feeling particularly grateful for anything, read back through your journal. Thank God for what he has done, for what he is doing, and for what he is going to do in the future. This simple activity will shift your focus to the good things in your life—to the blessings God is bringing your way. You'll begin to feel more joy. Your thankfulness will breed more to be thankful for. I challenge you to try keeping a gratitude journal for a couple months and see how it affects your daily attitude. I bet you'll be glad you did.

If the idea of journaling intimidates you, you may want to start with something smaller. Try writing a favorite scripture or a quotation about gratefulness on a sticky note and putting it on your bathroom mirror. While you brush your teeth or comb your hair, focus on that little piece of paper. You'll be reminded to pull back from the urgent concerns of the day and spend a few minutes giving attention to what you are grateful for. When you make choosing gratitude each morning a habit, you will see your level of thankfulness skyrocket. You will suddenly be more aware of the good things in your life, and this new focus will shape the contours of your days for the better. Before long, you'll find yourself waking up saying, "Good morning, Lord!" rather than "Good Lord, it's morning!"

## REMOVE ALL COMPLAINTS FROM YOUR LIFE.

As we've already established, people love to complain. They like the attention and sympathy it gets them. Like a dog licking a wound, the complainer feels better in the moment of complaining, but it only makes the actual problem worse. When you fuel the fire of a difficult situation or negative circumstance with words, the more severe the situation or circumstance becomes. Just as gratitude breeds more to be grateful for, complaints breed more to complain about.

> If you don't like something, change it. If you can't change it, change your attitude. Don't complain.
>
> Maya Angelou

To get the complaints out of your life, you have to realize why they are there to begin with. Complaining is a symptom of something deeper; it's a symptom of a life preoccupied with negativity—one caught in an energy-draining, destructive, self-perpetuating cycle of wrong focus, wrong thinking, and wrong words. Complaining is a slippery slope. One complaint leads to another, then to another after that. Before you know it, you're officially a complainer. That naturally invites other people to complain around you, which does nothing but lead to the creation of a cynical, destructive environment.

The best way to break the cycle of complaining and the problems it causes is to make a drastic change. Don't just try to cut down on complaining. Instead, make a decision to remove all complaints from your life. When you feel a complaint about to slip from your lips, shift your focus away from your problem to something you are grateful for. Get in the habit of turning your attention toward the good things in your life rather than harping on the bad. Take Paul's words to heart:

> Finally, brothers and sisters, whatever is true, whatever is noble, whatever is right, whatever is pure, whatever is lovely, whatever is admirable—if anything is excellent or praiseworthy—think about such things. (Phil. 4:8 NIV)

Paul understood the reality that our thoughts lead to words and that words lead to life or death. So he backs things up a step and warns us not only to not speak negativity, but not to even think on negative things. In the bestselling book *A Complaint Free World*, author Will Bowen put it this way:

> Think of your mind as a manufacturer and your mouth as a customer. The manufacturer produces negative thoughts that are purchased by the customer when they are expressed as complaints. It

goes like this: The manufacturer (your brain) produces a negative thought, which the customer (your
mouth) purchases by complaining. If the customer
will stop buying what the manufacturer produces,
the manufacturer will retool. When you stop complaining about what you perceive to be wrong and
begin to speak about what you are grateful for and
what you desire, you force your manufacturer brain
to develop a new product line.[1]

What if you were to make a decision to stop complaining for just
one week? For seven days, choose to intentionally move your focus
away from everything that's wrong in your world and concentrate
instead on the good that surrounds you. Focus on God and what he
has done for you. Don't allow a complaint to escape your lips. You'll
be amazed at what will happen in your life during that week simply
because you chose to lay negativity aside and shift your attention
toward gratefulness.

## BE QUICK TO SAY "THANK YOU."

There are two different levels of gratefulness you should be quick to
express to the people in your life. The first is simple common courtesy. When someone does something nice for you, say thank you.
Don't take kindness for granted. More important, though, make a
point of saying thank you to the people who influence your life on
a larger scale—those who pour into you and help you walk through
the world in step with the best version of yourself. Who is that
for you? Who has impacted your life in a significant way? There is

tremendous power in thanking them for what they've done, even when—especially when—they don't realize they've done anything at all.

During my final year of undergrad, my university started a program to encourage deliberate expressions of gratitude. Students who met certain academic criteria were invited to an end-of-year banquet. Each qualifying student was encouraged to invite a teacher from his or her high school years who had been particularly influential. The university wanted to make these individuals guests of honor at the banquet so that we, the students—now on the cusp of graduating from the next phase—could thank them for their early impact on our lives.

When I found out I qualified for the banquet, I knew immediately that I wanted to invite my high school biology teacher, Mr. Sylvester. Even though I had hated biology, I loved Mr. Sylvester. He was always challenging me to rise to new levels. He regularly pushed me to achieve more than I thought I could and taught me important lessons about meeting life head on. Out of all the teachers I'd encountered, he had definitely had the most impact on my life.

Unfortunately, the timing wasn't good. Mr. Sylvester's wife was sick, and he didn't feel comfortable making the trip. I was disappointed he couldn't be at the banquet, but even more than that, I didn't want to waste the opportunity I'd been given to thank him for his influence. So I sat down and wrote a letter filled with what I would have said to him in person if I'd had the chance. After I dropped the letter in the mail, life got busy, and I didn't think much about it—or about Mr. Sylvester—for the next several years.

Ten years after my college graduation, I was visiting my hometown and had lunch with an old friend, who happened to be Mr. Sylvester's son. When I asked how his dad was doing, my friend's face fell. Apparently, things weren't great in Mr. Sylvester's life. He had lost his wife years ago, and now his own health was failing. But as my friend described some of the difficulties his dad had been facing, he said, "I want you to know how much that letter you sent to him meant. He framed it and hung it on the wall in his office." My friend went on to say that from time to time his dad would point to my letter and make a comment about how his forty years of teaching had made a difference. I was blown away that my small gesture had meant so much to him.

Everyone wants to matter. Everyone wants to know they are making a difference. When we fail to say thank you to the people who have had an impact on our lives, we are robbing them of the sense of joy and fulfillment that could so easily be theirs. Never assume others know how you feel; say it. They may hope they have touched your life in some way, but they won't know for sure until you tell them.

Using your words to let someone know his or her life has made a difference is the single best way to impact that individual positively in return. Those words create a ripple effect. When you speak gratitude into the life of someone who has influenced you, you literally shift that person's perspective. You ignite a reaction that not only bolsters his or her self-perception, but you also make that person want to continue giving. Whether or not he or she goes on to influence others could hinge on whether that person hears a thank you from you. Your words have that kind of power. Put them to use.

## *LEARN TO LIVE EVERY DAY IN A STATE OF PRESENT JOY.*

Have you ever met someone who is always waiting for life's next milestone before he or she can be happy? Maybe you are one of those people. I have a close friend who does this all the time. When we were in school, he couldn't wait to graduate because then he would be happy. After graduation, he couldn't wait to meet the right woman and get married because he had decided that's when life would truly start. After he got married, he began focusing on moving up the ladder in his company. He felt like each successive rung would be the one to finally give him a sense of "making it." Then kids became the missing ingredient that he couldn't be happy without, so he and his wife decided to start a family. To this day, every time I talk to him, there's some new milestone on the horizon that he thinks will finally make him content.

Being content doesn't mean we shouldn't have dreams for the future. But as we plan, set goals, and work toward them, we need to live in the present with a sense of peace and gratitude. Take a look at the attitude Paul models in his letter to the Philippians:

> I have learned to be content whatever the circum-
> stances. I know what it is to be in need, and I know
> what it is to have plenty. I have learned the secret of
> being content in any and every situation, whether
> well fed or hungry, whether living in plenty or in
> want. (Phil. 4:11–12 NIV)

We all have a tendency to overlook the joy in everyday life because we are so focused on the weekend, next month's vacation, our next relationship, our next promotion, or whatever we think will finally make us content. When you and I constantly give our attention to what's to come rather than what is, we aren't really living; we're wishing away our lives minute by minute, hour by hour, day by day, year by year. Life has to be lived in the now. If we don't learn how to be grateful for the realities of the mundane, we are never going to truly live. We'll get to the end of life and realize that we've simply existed, waiting and wishing our way from one thing to the next.

> We usually lose today, because there has been a yesterday, and tomorrow is coming.
>
> Goethe

Words have the power to end this cycle of discontentment. Using them to build an attitude of gratitude will draw you into a deeper appreciation of life's day-to-day beauty. That attitude is what will keep you from looking back one day and wishing you could relive the last ten, twenty, or thirty years being more present. How can you get started? Make the decision to hold your tongue when you start to say things such as:

> "I can't wait until Friday."
> "If only my vacation would hurry up and get here."
> "Is it five o'clock yet?"
> "When will I find my partner in life?"
> "Will I ever get to live in a place I really love?"
> "When _____ happens, I'll finally be happy."

Instead of speaking want, develop a habit of focusing on what you are grateful for in the moment. Thank God for his goodness, for your health, for your family and friends, for the ability to work and create income. Thank him for giving you another day of life and a purpose to fulfill. Thank him for putting people around you whom you can encourage and help grow into the best versions of themselves. Thank him for giving you the opportunity to get better every day in every way and to continually draw closer to him. If you are having a hard time focusing on present joy, try meditating on King David's words:

> Shout with joy to the LORD, all the earth!
>> Worship the LORD with gladness.
>> Come before him, singing with joy.
> Acknowledge that the LORD is God!
>> He made us, and we are his.
>> We are his people, the sheep of his pasture.
> Enter his gates with thanksgiving;
>> go into his courts with praise.
>> Give thanks to him and praise his name.
> For the LORD is good.
>> His unfailing love continues forever,
>> and his faithfulness continues to each
>>> generation. (Ps. 100)

If you'll simply start looking, you'll find countless things to be thankful for. Think about those things. Talk about those things. Let your subconscious hear your grateful words so it can, in turn, foster more opportunities for gratefulness in your life.

As you begin working these practices into your day, you will start seeing all you have to be grateful for with fresh eyes. Your heart will begin to shift toward an appreciation for the good in your life, and your words will reflect that shift. You'll begin exuding a new attitude that will make you happier and that others will notice. Not only will this growth enhance your own life, but it will also help to spur gratitude in those around you, thereby elevating their lives. Once again, you have the opportunity to be the catalyst to a better life for yourself and the people you love. It all begins with saying *thank you.*

*Chapter 7*

# THE ART OF CURSING

**(Warning: This chapter is rated PG-13.)**

*My father worked in profanity the way other artists might*
*work in oils or clay. It was his true medium, a master.*

Ralphie *(A Christmas Story)*


*Don't use foul or abusive language. Let everything*
*you say be good and helpful, so that your words will*
*be an encouragement to those who hear them.*

Paul (Eph. 4:29)


A few years ago, I was standing in the buffet line at a lunch meeting hosted by a close friend. A woman I've known for almost a decade had also been invited to the meeting. She was just ahead of me in line, and we chit-chatted as we fixed our plates. She was one of the sweetest women I've ever known. Think typical Southern, church-going grandmother. This woman's husband had been sick, so she was fixing his plate along with hers as she worked her way down the buffet. Just as she made it to the desserts, she lost her grip on one of the now-full plates, and in her quick attempt to catch it, both plates crashed to the floor. As the food ricocheted off the tile, a loud curse word ricocheted from her lips. Everyone within earshot went wide-eyed and then chuckled under their breath as her hand flew to her mouth in embarrassment.

Now, my ears are not sensitive to cursing. As I've already mentioned, I grew up thinking cursing was a competition and trying my best to be the winner. Plus, there are plenty of people I know who flippantly use my sweet friend's word of choice many times every day. If I'd heard it from one of them, there would have been no shock factor at all. But coming from her, a curse of any kind was so unexpected that it resonated in a different way. While cursing is an issue I had wrestled with extensively in the past, something about the irony of my plate-dropping friend's potty mouth got me thinking more deeply about curse words—how they got their designation, where they're rooted in all of us, and why it matters whether or not we say them.

## UNDERSTANDING THE CURSE BEHIND CURSE WORDS

Have you ever wondered how certain words became taboo? Why is it cursing to put an *i* between the letters *s*, *h*, and *t*, but it's okay to put *oo* in there? Why do kids on the playground get in trouble for *h*, *e*, double hockey sticks, but people talking about heaven and hell can say it with no problem? The late comedian George Carlin hit a nerve with the American public in the early 1970s by diving into questions like these in his stand-up routine *Seven Words You Can Never Say on Television*. Carlin took a tongue-in-cheek look at some words it's okay to say some of the time but not all of the time, as he put it. His point was that you can never be quite sure what words are on the elusive don't-say list, because everybody's list is different. Since we've all wrestled with what we can say versus what we can't say, and in front of whom, the bit was wildly popular. After all, what really constitutes cursing? Is the answer the same in every context?

While there is a cultural element to what's accepted as clean speech, the answer to how curse words became curse words and which words qualify dates back to the days of Adam and Eve. Take a look at this account of the infamous forbidden fruit incident:

> The serpent was the shrewdest of all the wild ani-mals the LORD God had made. One day he asked the woman, "Did God really say you must not eat the fruit from any of the trees in the garden?"

> "Of course we may eat fruit from the trees in the garden," the woman replied. "It's only the fruit from the tree in the middle of the garden that we are not allowed to eat. God said: 'You must not eat it or even touch it; if you do, you will die.'"

> "You won't die!" the serpent replied to the woman. "God knows that your eyes will be opened as soon as you eat it, and you will be like God, knowing both good and evil."

> The woman was convinced. She saw that the tree was beautiful and its fruit looked delicious, and she wanted the wisdom it would give her. So she took some of the fruit and ate it. Then she gave some

to her husband, who was with her, and he ate it, too. At that moment their eyes were opened, and they suddenly felt shame at their nakedness. So they sewed fig leaves together to cover themselves.

When the cool evening breezes were blowing, the man and his wife heard the LORD God walking about in the garden. So they hid from the LORD God among the trees. Then the LORD God called to the man, "Where are you?"

He replied, "I heard you walking in the garden, so I hid. I was afraid because I was naked."

"Who told you that you were naked?" the LORD God asked. "Have you eaten from the tree whose fruit I commanded you not to eat?"

The man replied, "It was the woman you gave me who gave me the fruit, and I ate it."

Then the LORD God asked the woman, "What have you done?"

"The serpent deceived me," she replied. "That's why I ate it."

Then the LORD God said to the serpent,

"Because you have done this, you are cursed
    more than all animals, domestic and wild.
You will crawl on your belly,
    groveling in the dust as long as you live.
And I will cause hostility between you and the
        woman,
    and between your offspring and her offspring.
He will strike your head,
    and you will strike his heel." (Gen. 3:1–15)

The words you and I know as curse words today have their root in the curse that God put on the serpent in the garden of Eden. Here's a little background you may or may not already be familiar with: Before the creation of the world, Satan was one of God's angels. But because of Satan's pride and unfaithfulness, God cast him and some of his cohorts out of heaven. Thus began the battle between good and evil that rages to this day. When Adam and Eve came on the scene, Satan saw a great opportunity to turn God's own creation against him. So he took on the form of a serpent and slithered into his role as the tempter. But God recognized Satan's schemes and put a curse on him during their exchange in the garden. In the broader sense, when God cursed the serpent, he cursed all of sin. Every incarnation of sin is under that curse, as is anyone who willfully chooses to sin.

In our day, we like to talk about Major League Baseball curses and black magic curses that are levied on unsuspecting victims, but these types of so-called curses have no basis. The power people try to give them exists merely in the human realm. God is the only one who can curse something; true curses are completely under his control. And the only thing God curses is sin, or unfaithfulness to him. When you and I choose unfaithfulness, we step outside the realm of his blessing. Or to think of it another way, we step under the cloud of his curse. Now, that doesn't mean God is out to get you if you aren't living by his principles. He's not in the business of flinging active curses on people. Rather, the curse is more passive; he may simply choose not to bless you in the same way he would if you were being faithful. When you choose faithfulness, that cloud of cursing lifts, and you are back in God's blessing zone. (For a more in-depth theological examination of active versus passive curses, go to TonguePierced.com.)

Curse words, as they have existed for thousands of years and as you and I know them today, are verbal expressions of unfaithfulness that have grown directly out of the curse God put on sin. They are key players in the ongoing battle for control of your heart and mine. When you slip into cursing, even flippantly, you are letting words of death and destruction overtake words of life. Such words can only undermine your own best interests and hurt the people around you.

I've observed something interesting over the years: People who are walking closest with Jesus generally have the purest speech. Not to say they won't slip in a curse word on occasion—like the plate-dropping grandmother—but as a rule, their language reflects a God-directed heart. In other words, the level of your language is a good indicator of how intimate your relationship with God is. Now, let me be clear; this isn't a legalism issue. There's nothing you can do to make God love you more or that could cause him to love you less.

How frequently you do or don't let a curse word escape from your lips doesn't earn you brownie points or give you black marks in his eyes. It's the other way around. Pure language isn't a requirement of a close walk with God; it's a result.

## CURBING THE CURSE

At its core, getting curse words out of your life is an internal process that will begin to happen as you invite Jesus to take control of your heart and then bring your mind and your words into alignment with what he is doing in you. Don't forget the principle of organic consistency from chapter 2. That said, there are some practical steps you can begin taking to get destructive, unfaithful words out of your vocabulary, even as you allow him to begin working in you and through you.

### 1. BE AWARE OF THE TRUTH ABOUT CURSING.

Like so much of language, cursing is often a learned behavior. In college, I knew a guy who had grown up in a conservative Southern household where there was virtually no cursing. He told me that if he ever heard any curses, they were on the light side—definitely no f-bombs. The word just wasn't culturally acceptable. When he got to college freshman year, he ended up in a dorm room with a nice guy from New Jersey. They had a lot in common and got along well, but one thing blew my friend's mind: f-bombs saturated his new room-mate's language. This guy made an art form out of the word, melding it to mean a myriad of different things and using it in all kinds of ways—even when talking to his parents on the phone.

The most striking thing was that the word didn't seem to mean anything to him. He had grown up with it in the air. His parents used it freely. His friends had always said it, as had their parents. So he did too. This word that was so taboo to my friend was practically no stronger than *darn* or *shoot* to his new roommate. Their opposing associations with the word were completely cultural—but neither perception was based on the truth about cursing. My friend didn't avoid the word because he was walking in faithfulness to God, and his roommate didn't say it because he wasn't. Still, the clean speech habits my friend had learned growing up ultimately helped him see the truth about cursing more quickly than his roommate.

In a letter to believers in the ancient city of Ephesus, Paul wrote, "Don't use foul or abusive language" (Eph. 4:29). But, really, what's the big deal? If the motivation is innocent enough, then what difference does it make if someone uses the f-bomb to express himself or something more delicate? The answer lies in the true nature of cursing.

Curse words fall into two categories. First, there are the expressions that use God's name in vain. Scripture is clear that God's name shouldn't be tossed around flippantly, which makes both GD and using Jesus's name as a glib exclamation off-limits for anyone wanting to use words in a way that honor and reflect him:

> You must not misuse the name of the Lord your
> God. The Lord will not let you go unpunished if
> you misuse his name. (Exod. 20:7)

The second category is mostly made up of words that are historically connected to either crude sexuality or biological functions like waste elimination. While these words don't carry the same weight, they are still under and reflective of the curse. They're in no way beneficial to the one saying them. All curses—even my friend's roommate's nonchalant f-bombs—are human attempts to play God, even if the curser doesn't realize it. They are attempts to do something that only God can do.

Consider another example: Say you've been slaving away over a big project at work for months. Then, when the day comes to present it to the higher-ups, your boss takes the credit for everything you've done. Do you mutter something under your breath? Do you call him the offspring of a female dog? What you are really doing when you curse him, whether you intend to or not, is trying to play God in his life. You are, in essence, attempting to control his identity and destiny. But God is the only one who can do that.

Or consider this scenario: You're moving into a new place and decide to hang some pictures. You position a nail on the wall, draw back the hammer, and accidentally hit your thumb with the first blow. What might you say? *Damn it* is a pretty common exclamation in this situation. But what are you damning? You're not damning your thumb; it wasn't your thumb's fault it got hit. You're probably not damning the nail, unless it fell and caused the problem. You're damning the hammer. Think about how foolish that is. First of all, you are speaking a curse on an inanimate object. A hammer can't be damned. Even if it could, you don't have the power to damn anything. So what's the point in speaking that kind of worthless curse?

Maybe you'll concede that one, but you think a word like the s-word is more neutral. Well, not really. Consider its history:

The s-word, as we use it today, came into our language at the time of the bubonic plague. It was a way to say to another person, "I hope you get the plague and die." Talk about a human attempt to curse another person. To throw around the s-word like it's nothing is actually to throw around a word whose history is rooted in a deadly form of poor intent. Even if that's not how you think about it today, the etymology is undeniable. You can't just claim ignorance and change the substance of the word to fit your linguistic desires.

If you play out this kind of scenario with every curse word, you're going to realize that using them in daily conversation is pointless—even laughable. You can't put a curse on someone. You can't play God in someone else's life. When you throw around curse words, at best you are inadvertently cursing something that can't be or doesn't need to be cursed in the first place. At worst, you are using your words to set yourself up as a little god, instead of using them to love the one true God. Remember James's assertion:

> [The tongue] is restless and evil, full of deadly poison. Sometimes it praises our Lord and Father, and sometimes it curses those who have been made in the image of God. And so blessing and cursing come pouring out of the same mouth. Surely, my brothers and sisters, this is not right! (James 3:8–10)

Cursing is a major component of the deadly poison that James mentions. Like all words, curse words' creative force will shape your world. Making them part of your habitual speech is like drinking a small dose of poison each day; it probably won't kill you, but it's definitely going to leave you weaker and less healthy. Not only does cursing tint your own perception of the world, but it also negatively influences others' opinions about you. For example, statistics show that people who curse in the workplace don't get promoted as often as those who don't curse. As a contributor to Forbes.com recently noted,

> 64% of employers said that they'd think less of an employee who repeatedly uses curse words, and 57% would be less likely to promote that person....
>
> A majority of hiring managers said they believe that the use of curse words brings the employee's professionalism into question, while others are concerned with the lack of control and lack of maturity demonstrated by swearing at work. More than half said using dirty words at work makes an employee appear less intelligent.[1]

There's an off-putting air about foul language—one that leads to negative perceptions. Regardless of their historical context, you and I can argue that the words don't mean anything to us and try to defend our right to say whatever we please, but deep down we know that curses are attached to a heavy weight; deep down we know that the better choice would be to avoid cursing altogether. Something within our spirit understands that keeping curse words around puts unnecessary space between our current reality and God's best.

## 2. THINK BEFORE YOU SPEAK.

Have you ever heard the story of the fly that lived on a cow farm in Indiana? One day the fly was particularly hungry. As he was buzzing around looking for some food, he saw his favorite meal—a big, fresh cow patty. Excited by his discovery, the little fly dove in and feasted until he could feast no more. But when he tried to fly away, he realized there was a problem. He had eaten so much that he was too heavy for his wings to lift him off the ground. What's a fly to do? Well, this enterprising little sucker spotted a broom leaning against the wall of the barn. He came up with a plan. The fly decided to climb to the top of the broom and jump off, assuming that once he was in the air with his wings spread, he'd be able to fly.

The little hero waddled over to the broom and grunted his way to the tip of the handle. Once as high as he could go, he catapulted himself off and flapped his wings with all his might. But he was still too heavy to fly. He fell to the ground with a splat—and that was the end of Mr. Fly. The moral of the story? Don't fly off the handle when you're full of crap. In other words, think before you speak.

Thinking before you speak is easier said than done, but it's a habit worth working into your life. Thoughtless words can do an immense amount of damage. When you lash out in the heat of the moment, without taking the time to consider what the implication of your words will be, you are more likely to say something you'll regret. If you are in an emotional situation—if your feelings are hurt, if you're angry, if you feel threatened—you're going to have a harder time choosing your words well. And you're more likely to revert to curses. Heated emotions and curse words tend to go together like, well, like flies and cow patties.

Once thoughtless words come spewing out of your mouth, you can't get them back. An impression has been made. The damage has been done. Those words are out there, busily creating their corresponding reality. This truth doesn't just apply to spoken words either. So many people hurt themselves and others by shooting off an angry email or text message before thinking through the consequences. Once sent, those harmful words are physically available for the recipient to read, reread, and hold on to for posterity. Perhaps even more than spoken words, written words of anger hurt relationships and lead to unnecessary pain. Even if you feel like they are justified in the moment, they never do anything to make a situation better. The only thing that can do that is to learn to think before you speak and to choose words that have the potential to restore life. Proverbs 15:23 speaks to this truth:

> Everyone enjoys a fitting reply; it is wonderful to
> say the right thing at the right time!

With a little intentionality, you can learn to say the right thing at the right time, no matter what kind of situation you're in—whether it's a calm, everyday conversation or a highly emotional exchange. All you have to do is pause and consider.

## Pause

Never respond immediately in a situation where you're emotionally invested. Before you say those words you're just itching to say—those words that would prove your point and put the other person in her place—pause. Put some space between the stimulus and your response so you can counter in the right way. Instead of lashing out with curses, hurtful names, or accusations, intentionally hold your tongue for a minute, no matter how hard it is or how right you think you are.

If what you want to say in the heat of the moment is justified and something the person on the receiving end needs to hear, then it will still be the right thing to say in an hour, a day, or even a week, whereas lashing out with thoughtless, hateful, or unfair words in a moment of emotion could lead to a host of bad consequences. You could destroy a relationship and your reputation in one fell swoop—not to mention cause significant, likely undeserved damage to the person you're talking to. Pausing before you speak is always worth the discipline it requires. It will never ultimately stop you from saying the right thing, but it can always protect you from saying the wrong.

## Consider

As you learn to pause, use that space to consider whether or not the words that are about to come out of your mouth would please God. Ask yourself whether you would still say them if Jesus were standing right beside you. In the Psalms, David wrote,

> May the words of my mouth and the meditation of
> my heart be pleasing to you, O LORD, my rock and
> my redeemer. (19:14)

You already understand the importance of taking your thoughts captive. In the same way, you have to capture the words that are trying to rush ahead of those thoughts. Choosing to consider their worth and implications before they escape your lips will have a radical impact on your conversations with the people in your life. It will save relationships that might otherwise be destroyed and make already healthy relationships even stronger. Filtering your words through the prism of what would be pleasing to God is the best way to make sure they are a blessing and not a curse.

## 3. TAKE DRASTIC ACTION.

When you're standing at the edge of a cold ocean, wishing you were already in up to your chest bobbing with the waves, what's the best way to get there? Is it easiest to edge into the water a little bit at a time or to bite the bullet and throw yourself under? Most people would agree that diving in is easier than tiptoeing. Before you know it, you're used to the chill and happily splashing around.

The best path to ousting an old habit and establishing a new one is strikingly similar. When you want to initiate a shift, the key is to commit to drastic change for a set period of time. Then the old habit will be lost to the comfort of your new reality. Since using curse words as you navigate through the world is largely a bad habit, the best way to nip the habit is to become aware of the truth about those words, learn to pause and consider before you speak, and take drastic action to eliminate them from your vocabulary. In other words, quit cold turkey.

If I challenged you to go thirty days without saying a curse word, do you think you could do it? Where you're starting from will determine the level of difficulty. If you've never been much of a curser, you may already go thirty days at a time without any profanity slipping through your lips. On the other hand, if this is something you've struggled to get under control or never considered to be an issue until these pages, you may have a harder time cleaning up your language—but it will be worth it. Since the tongue-pierced lifestyle is characterized by using your words to love God and love others, then getting the words that trace back to the curse out of your life is a foundational step.

So here's my challenge to you: I challenge you to strip all curse words from your speech for thirty days. If you slip, start the thirty days over. When you want to curse, simply keep your mouth closed or choose to replace those words with something more life-giving. If you start questioning whether one word or another is actually a curse word, then it is. When in doubt, don't say it. By the time you go thirty consecutive days without cursing, the habit will be broken, and you'll be steeped in a new, more productive way of speaking. You will have eliminated some of the most negative, heaviest weight-carrying culprits from your vocabulary.

This isn't about becoming a Goody Two-Shoes or trying to portray a certain image. Again, the issue is not a legalistic one. You can't earn God's love by obeying rules:

> But those who depend on the law to make them right with God are under his curse, for the Scriptures say, "Cursed is everyone who does not observe and obey all the commands that are written in God's Book of the Law." So it is clear that no one can be made right with God by trying to keep the law. For the Scriptures say, "It is

through faith that a righteous person has life."
(Gal. 3:10–11)

Rather, the thirty-day no-cursing challenge is about intentionally ridding your life of something that has no power to foster
anything but a poor attitude, negativity, and destruction. As you
stop cursing, your inner ear will adjust to not hearing those words.
With some time and effort, and as you continually surrender control of your heart to God, they'll stop coming to your mind with
such frequency. Simply by making the decision to bring your words
more in line with God's, you'll be stepping toward faithfulness;
you'll feel more of his peace and love in your life—and you'll reflect
more of that peace and love to the people around you.

# THE THIRTY-DAY NO-CURSING CHALLENGE

## CHALLENGE

Go thirty consecutive days without saying a curse word. If you slip, start over.

## TIPS FOR SUCCESS:

- Remind yourself of the truth about cursing often.
- Pause and consider your words before you speak them.
- When a curse word is on the tip of your tongue, remain silent.
- Shift your focus to something positive you can say—and say that instead.
- If you aren't sure whether something is a curse word or not, it is.
- Ask God to help you bring his thoughts to your words.
- Memorize Ephesians 4:29 and Psalm 19:14. Repeat them to yourself often:

- Don't use foul or abusive language. Let everything you say be good and helpful, so that your words will be an encouragement to those who hear them. (Eph. 4:29)
- May the words of my mouth and the meditation of my heart be pleasing to you, O LORD, my rock and my redeemer. (Ps. 19:14)

As the old adage goes, a rising tide raises all ships. Cursing is so prevalent in our culture that when your language is clean, the people around you notice. And since it's uncomfortable to curse around someone who doesn't, those same people will start to mirror cleaner language back to you. If you don't believe me, just give it a try, and watch what happens. At worst, their cleaner language will do nothing but bolster the quality of their lives from the outside in. At best, it will open a discussion about the true root and destructive nature of cursing and begin moving them toward an inside-out, tongue-pierced lifestyle as well. Cursing may be an art form to some, but a life spent speaking words of truth and light results in a much more nuanced, more beautiful masterpiece.

Chapter 8

# MASTERING CONFRONTATION AND CONFLICT

*Whenever you're in conflict with someone,*
*there is one factor that can make the difference*
*between damaging your relationship and deepening it.*
*That factor is attitude.*

William James

*Wounds from a friend can be trusted,*
*but an enemy multiplies kisses.*

King Solomon (Prov. 27:6 NIV)

I spent about a decade of my life living in Manhattan. While most stereotypes about New Yorkers are just that—stereotypes—there is one arguably beneficial quality among northeastern city dwellers that lives up to its reputation: As a rule, they are more open to confrontation and conflict than people in many other parts of the country. There's a certain brashness, a bolder mind-set. When New Yorkers see a wrong, they are usually quick to say something about it—whether they've ever met the person they are confronting or not. The only problem is that the motivation, and therefore the end result of the confrontation, isn't always what it should be.

While you and I can learn a lot from this fearlessness in the face of confrontation and conflict, it needs to be tempered with a proper understanding of what the goal of healthy confrontation really is: restoring godliness where it has been lost. Consider this definition of healthy confrontation:

> *Healthy Confrontation*—A healthy confrontation is
> a meeting between two friends for the purpose of
> restoring godliness.

Notice the two parts of the definition. First, healthy confrontation happens between people who care about each other. It may be between friends, family members, or coworkers, as long as the two people in the confrontation know and respect each other. Someone who isn't a friend has no reason to listen to anything you have to say. You haven't earned the right to speak into his or her life, so a confrontation of any kind will likely just deteriorate into an argument or be ignored altogether.

Second, healthy confrontation is geared toward a specific purpose—restoring godliness. This is a critical part of the definition. You shouldn't confront someone just because she has offended you in some way or because you think she needs to change her behavior. The impetus has to be deeper. Healthy confrontation can only happen when the need for it grows out of something that is a sin in God's eyes. The goal of a healthy confrontation isn't to elicit an apology for you or to get someone to live more in line with the way you think she should; it's to help the person you're confronting realign herself with God's best.

In many of our vocabularies, confrontation and conflict are negative words. We think of them as uncomfortable encounters that we'd rather avoid. But when confrontation, and the potential resulting conflict, is entered into between two people who care about each other for the purpose of restoring godliness, it is a pathway to good. Healthy confrontation is an opportunity to use your words to bring life to a broken situation or to a struggling loved one. If you and I can take a seed of that city boldness and marry it to the heart of thoughtful intervention, we can engage in necessary confrontation and conflict with less fear and better results.

## THE ART OF CONFRONTATION

Speaking of fear, are you scared of confrontation? In today's please-all culture—and especially in Christian circles—most people are. We're afraid that if we speak up, we might offend someone, that the person we want to call out might get mad at us or that we'll look foolish or judgmental. While those things are possibilities, they shouldn't keep us from stepping into necessary, healthy confrontations. A study of Jesus's life shows that he was never afraid to confront people when they needed confronting. He did it boldly, but with love and always for the ultimate purpose of restoring godliness. There's an art to this kind of confrontation—both to knowing when it should happen and how to go about it.

While a good one, Jesus isn't the only example we can turn to when it comes to determining whether a confrontation is called for and crafting the right approach. Long before Jesus was born, a prophet named Nathan confronted King David during his reign over Israel. The confrontation was so effective that it has served as a model for healthy confrontations for the thousands of years since. To understand the power and practicalities of Nathan's confrontation, consider these important points about the context:

- As a young man, David was a shepherd. During that time, he had an encounter with Goliath and became the most famous underdog victor in all of history. After that, he was chosen to be the future king of Israel.

- David's initial reign over Israel was a period of unprecedented peace and prosperity for the region. To this day, he's still considered one of the most effective kings in all of history.

- One morning, while David was walking on the roof of his house, he saw a woman bathing on a nearby rooftop. He took a liking to her, had her brought to him, and committed adultery with her. The two began a long-term affair, which resulted in her becoming pregnant. To cover his tracks, David sent Bathsheba's husband to the front lines of a battle where he would likely be killed, and he was. So in a short period of time, the upstanding king had gotten off course, to say the least—he had become an adulterer, fathered a child out of wedlock, and had a man killed.

- Nathan and David were friends. They had a lot of trust and shared experience between them. Given their history and his role as a spiritual leader of the day, Nathan felt a need to confront David about the situation he had gotten himself into.

Godliness clearly needed to be restored. Cue a healthy confrontation:

So the LORD sent Nathan the prophet to tell David this story: "There were two men in a certain town. One was rich, and one was poor. The rich man owned a great many sheep and cattle. The poor man owned nothing but one little lamb he had bought. He raised that little lamb, and it grew up with his children. It ate from the man's own plate and drank from his cup. He cuddled it in his arms like a baby daughter. One day a guest arrived at the home of the rich man. But instead of killing an animal from his own flock or herd, he took the poor man's lamb and killed it and prepared it for his guest."

David was furious. "As surely as the LORD lives," he vowed, "any man who would do such a thing deserves to die! He must repay four lambs to the poor man for the one he stole and for having no pity."

Then Nathan said to David, "You are that man! The LORD, the God of Israel, says: I anointed you king of Israel and saved you from the power of Saul. I gave you your master's house and his wives and the kingdoms of Israel and Judah. And if that had not been enough, I would have given you much, much more. Why, then, have you despised the word of the LORD and done this horrible deed? For you have murdered Uriah the Hittite with the sword of the Ammonites and stolen his wife. From this time on, your family will live by the sword because you have despised me by taking Uriah's wife to be your own...."

Then David confessed to Nathan, "I have sinned against the LORD."

Nathan replied, "Yes, but the LORD has forgiven you, and you won't die for this sin. Nevertheless, because you have shown utter contempt for the LORD by doing this, your child will die." (2 Sam. 12:1–10, 13–14)

You and I aren't prophets and probably won't be rubbing shoulders with a king anytime soon. Still, there are five practicalities we can glean from Nathan's confrontation of David to help us engage in more effective, healthy confrontation when it's called for.

## FIVE STEPS TO LIFE-GIVING CONFRONTATION

### 1. FOLLOW GOD'S LEAD.

Before you confront anyone, make sure God is the one leading you into the encounter. In other words, don't jump too quickly. Notice the first line of Nathan and David's story: "So the LORD sent Nathan." Confrontation isn't something you should decide to do flippantly or without a lot of forethought and prayer. In fact, when you think you need to confront someone, the wisest thing you can do is to pause and critically evaluate whether or not a confrontation is truly the best course of action. Often, it's not. I've found that about 80 percent of the time when people think they need to confront another person, the confrontation isn't actually needed. When you make yourself part of that statistic, you cause unnecessary hurt and strife.

One of the best ways to tell whether or not God is leading you is to check your excitement level. If you are excited about confronting another person, there's a problem. Engaging in this kind of conflict with someone you care about should fill you with a healthy sense of dread. If you are looking forward to it, you're probably on a mission to prove yourself right and the other person wrong, likely looking out more for your own interests than for the interests of the person you want to face off with. When you read the account of Nathan's confrontation with David, there is absolutely no sense of excitement. He wasn't interested in proving a point or making himself feel like a better person. He engaged in the confrontation solely because God was leading him to speak truth into David's life.

Granted, sometimes it's hard to discern whether God is leading you into a confrontation or whether you have cooked up the need for it in your own mind. Here are a few questions you can ask to help you figure it out:

**Question 1: Is the person you think you need to confront dishonoring God?** In other words, is he behaving in a way that would make people think less of God? If what he's doing is confusing God's message or marring his name, then it may very well be time for a confrontation.

**Question 2: Are the person's actions damaging your relationship?** Is what the other person is doing creating a divide between the two of you? Here's the tricky part you have to consider before entering into a confrontation: The confrontation itself could potentially end the relationship. Some people don't take well to being confronted and will never forgive you for calling them out—even if godliness is ultimately restored. Just another reason to make sure a confrontation is absolutely necessary before barreling ahead.

**Question 3: Are the person's actions hurting others?** Are other people being affected by what's going on? In King David's case, he wasn't only hurting himself and Bathsheba; he was also threatening the whole nation of Israel. With so much in jeopardy, Nathan couldn't keep quiet.

**Question 4: Is the person you want to confront hurting herself?** Does she seem to be self-destructing or spiraling out of control? Often, someone caught in a cycle of sin can't see the personal consequences that are piling up.

Don't even begin to move in the direction of a confrontation without asking and answering these four questions. As you do, be on the lookout for God's confirmation. If he truly wants you to confront someone, he will confirm it through prayer, the study of his Word, and/or other people. You can save yourself and others a lot of pain by slowing down and making sure you are following God's lead before entering into a confrontation.

If, after this step, you still feel like a confrontation is the best thing, then follow the next step, requesting a private meeting.

## 2. REQUEST A PRIVATE MEETING.

To be effective and have any hope of maintaining your relationship with the confronted, schedule a time to sit down with him privately. You can't conduct a healthy confrontation in the presence of other people. If you try to, you will rob the other person of the opportunity to be vulnerable and hear what you are saying. His first instinct will be self-preservation; he will automatically get defensive to save face in front of the other people.

When Nathan modeled this step by sitting down with David privately, he was foreshadowing Jesus's instruction:

> If another believer sins against you, go privately and
> point out the offense. (Matt. 18:15)

Now, if the person you're confronting refuses to hear you out, there are other measures you can take, as Jesus described later in Matthew 18, but start by sitting down for a one-on-one conversation.

## 3. PREPARE TO TACTFULLY SHARE YOUR THOUGHTS.

Once the meeting is scheduled, it's time for some prep work. First, do a little self-examination. Check your own heart. Are you in a position to confront your friend or loved one about the issue at hand? Or are you guilty of the same type of offense or of some other sin that could cloud your ability to see the situation clearly? Think about Jesus's words:

First get rid of the log in your own eye; then you
will see well enough to deal with the speck in your
friend's eye. (Matt. 7:5)

Ask yourself if you are the right person to be doing the confrontation, if you are in a place to be able to be objective and lead the situation to a positive resolution. If you feel like you are, then it's time to take your preparation to the next level by writing out what you want to say.

This is where the power of your words really kicks in. The words you choose when confronting another person will make or break the encounter, not to mention the situation as a whole and potentially your relationship with the other person. There's a lot riding on what comes out of your mouth. Before the meeting happens, sit down and write out exactly what you want to say. If you slip into finger pointing or negativity, redirect yourself toward constructive words that will bring life.

If you think written preparation is too much trouble, then circle back to step 1 and reconsider whether God is the one leading you into the confrontation. This is serious business. A healthy confrontation demands and deserves thorough written preparation. Taking this step will not only allow you to craft the confrontation in the way it should go; it will also serve as the final confirmation that the confrontation is necessary.

Not long ago, I felt the need to confront a friend of mine about an issue that had come between us. Trying to follow Nathan's lead, I started working through these steps. When I got to this one about preparation, I was tempted to skip the writing it out part. I had already thought through what I wanted to say; writing it all down seemed like a waste of time. But I did it anyway—and ended up being glad I did. As I made myself put my thoughts on paper, I came to the realization that I didn't need to confront my friend at all; what I really needed to do was to forgive him.

Writing is a clarifying exercise. Seeing the words that have been swirling in your head captured and pinned to a piece of paper or a screen often brings a new perspective. As Flannery O'Connor famously said, "I write because I don't know what I think until I read what I say." The simple act of writing out what you're thinking and feeling about your proposed confrontation will allow you to see the situation with fresh eyes. It may even make you realize that you can restore peace without having to go through an uncomfortable confrontation at all.

Relationships are messy; it's easy to get caught up in the chaos and think you need to approach others about something they've done when what you really need to do is be willing to make allowances for their weaknesses and mistakes. One of the ways God grows us is by putting us around other people who think differently than we do or rub us the wrong way. Instead of jumping toward confrontation with those people when they offend us or cause a problem, we may just need to step back and create some space for grace in the situation. As it turned out, that's exactly what I needed to do with my friend—something I would have realized too late had I not been willing to sit down and write out what I thought I wanted to say to him.

If you do want to move ahead with the confrontation, the exercise of writing out what you plan to say will help you choose your words in a way that will have the most impact. It will allow you to craft your approach in a manner that will most resonate with the person you are confronting; it will give you more leeway to be tactful and creative than speaking off the cuff will. Take another look at how Nathan couched the hard truth he needed to bring to David:

> So the LORD sent Nathan the prophet to tell David this story: "There were two men in a certain town. One was rich, and one was poor. The rich man owned a great many sheep and cattle. The poor man owned nothing but one little lamb he had bought. He raised that little lamb, and it grew up with his children. It ate from the man's own plate and drank from his cup. He cuddled it in his arms like a baby daughter. One day a guest arrived at the home of the rich man. But instead of killing an animal from his own flock or herd, he took the poor man's lamb and killed it and prepared it for his guest." (2 Sam. 12:1–4)

Nathan's preparation is obvious. He knew that David had once been a nurturing shepherd who took great pride in tending to his sheep. Given this history, Nathan chose to take an indirect approach in the confrontation, telling David a story about a rich man who killed a poor man's lamb. Nathan knew how much the story would disgust David. He knew that it would touch him on an emotional level and open his heart to hearing the rest of what Nathan needed to say.

## 4. TELL THE TRUTH COMPASSIONATELY, AND LEAVE THE REST TO GOD.

Like you and I would probably be, David was quick to judge the rich man in Nathan's story. He didn't realize that the account was a vehicle to help him grasp the impact of what he had done with Bathsheba and to her husband, Uriah. When David's emotions flared, Nathan turned everything around with the heavy truth:

> David was furious. "As surely as the LORD lives," he vowed, "any man who would do such a thing deserves to die! He must repay four lambs to the poor man for the one he stole and for having no pity."
>
> Then Nathan said to David, "You are that man! The LORD, the God of Israel, says: I anointed you king of Israel and saved you from the power of Saul. I gave you your master's house and his wives and the kingdoms of Israel and Judah. And if that had not been enough, I would have given you much, much more. Why, then, have you despised the word of the LORD and done this horrible deed? For you have murdered Uriah the Hittite with the sword of the Ammonites and stolen his wife. From this time on, your family will live by the sword because you have despised me by taking Uriah's wife to be your own." (2 Sam. 12:5–10)

Nathan didn't point a finger and say, "Look what you did, you wretch." Instead, he tactfully and compassionately led David into an understanding of the situation he had created for himself. Once he had said what he'd planned to say, he stopped talking. He closed his mouth and trusted God to do the restorative work in David's heart—and that's exactly what happened.

One of the easiest mistakes to make in a confrontation is to keep talking when you should get quiet. Once you've said what you wanted to say, fight the natural inclination to fill the awkward space with unnecessary words. They will just cloud what needs to happen in the critical moments after you've levied a hard truth. If God has truly led you into the confrontation, then he is at work in it. Rambling on and on because you're uncomfortable will only confuse what he's trying to do in the other person's heart. Restoring godliness is God's role in the encounter; he simply uses you and me as instruments to help pave the way.

Hopefully, as you trust God in the situation enough to stop talking and allow him to work, the person you are confronting will recognize the truth in your words and, like David, come to a place of repentance. When he does, don't take an attitude of "I told you so" or "I'm glad you finally see it my way." Instead, be quick to offer a soft place to fall.

## 5. OFFER GRACE AND SUPPORT.

Confrontation is not about rubbing someone's nose in what he or she has done wrong. It's not about positioning yourself as morally superior. Rather, it's about coming alongside the person who has gotten off course and using the power of your words to help steer her back in the right direction. If you're engaging in a confrontation with the right motivation, you'll be eager to offer grace and support as your loved one comes to an understanding of how she's hurt you, herself, or others. Paul's words apply here:

> Be happy with those who are happy, and weep with
> those who weep. (Rom. 12:15)

I feel sure that Nathan was right by David's side, weeping with him and supporting him as he faced the consequences of his sin in the weeks and months after the confrontation. That kind of compassionate grace is the natural outflow of a healthy confrontation conducted from a place of right motivation.

## FROM CONFRONTER TO CONFRONTED

When you and I think about confrontation, we naturally see ourselves in the role of the confronter. But what if you were the one who needed to be confronted? Do you have a Nathan in your life? Do you have someone you have allowed into your inner circle whom you trust enough to call you out if necessary? Would you be able to humble yourself enough to hear the words your Nathan had to say and to recognize the work God was trying to do through him? These are questions worth asking, because the day may very well come when you find yourself on the other side of the confrontational equation. How you respond will likely determine the course of your life from that point on.

David couldn't have been the David we know him as without having Nathan in his life. In the same way, you can't become all you want to be without trusted friends or family members in your life—without people who feel like there is an open line of communication with you, one that they can tap into if they see you getting off track. Those kinds of relationships don't happen by default. The words you choose to speak in your relationships with others every day either build or destroy the foundation of trust that a godly confrontation needs to stand on.

If you don't have any Nathans in your life right now, use your words to start developing one or two. If there's no one in your circle who could be a Nathan, start praying that God will send you someone with whom you can connect and grow. Then, be willing to engage that relationship. Speak words of life into it, and keep it moving in a positive direction. Build the trust that is ultimately necessary for a healthy confrontation—either as the confronter or the confronted.

As crucial as it is to have a Nathan around, consider this as well: God would prefer to restore godliness in your life directly, rather than through a confrontation. In other words, he wants to have such deep, open communication with you that he can be the one to steer you back on course if you start to veer away from his best plan. He may do it through that still, small voice you can hear when you take the time to listen in your conversations with him. He may do it as you read his Word. Either way, he'd like to be able to admonish you directly when you're wrong and know that you'll listen to him. Hebrews 12:5–6 reads,

> My child, don't make light of the LORD's discipline,
> and don't give up when he corrects you. For the
> LORD disciplines those he loves, and he punishes
> each one he accepts as his child.

But if you don't listen—or worse, if you hear him but refuse to respond to his correction—he will send someone else to help with the job. Your Nathan will step up, and you'll find yourself in the middle of your own confrontation.

Confrontation can be a powerful exercise for both the confronter and the confronted. But before you rush into a confrontation, make sure God is the one leading you. Reread this chapter, and follow all the steps above. Choose to be bold, humble, and prayerful all at the same time. Then use your words to bring life to the situation; let yourself be an instrument for restoration. As you do, you will be cooperating with God to help someone you love live in deeper relationship with him.

*Chapter 9*

# WORDS THAT LAST

*A vocabulary of truth and simplicity will be*
*of service throughout your life.*

Winston Churchill

*Every one of these careless words is going*
*to come back to haunt you.*
*There will be a time of Reckoning. Words*
*are powerful; take them seriously.*
*Words can be your salvation. Words can also be your damnation.*

Jesus (Matt. 12:36–37 MSG)

Early in my college days, some members of my class and I took a trip to Mississippi for a steamboat ride on the river. The girth and force of the great waterway was something to behold. As the guide on our boat talked about the history of the river and detailed its modern stats and functions, I was struck by a thought that has never quite left me: The current of that river—and of every river in the world—continually shapes and reshapes the landmass around it. As it rolls over rocks and pushes against banks day after day after day, its never-ending flow forms those stones and that earth into their current state of being.

So it is with the stream of words that pours from your mouth on a daily basis. How you direct its flow week after week, month after month, year after year will define the contours of your very existence. Your word choices will determine the topography of your life—where the rough spots are, where there's smooth stone, and where the course bends in one direction or another. And the most interesting thing is that you won't even see it happening. Just as the water of the Mississippi changes the contours of its bank ever so slightly over time, the overall quality of your words shifts and reshapes the boundary lines of your life incrementally. While most of the effects are hard to see from day to day, over the course of many decades, the words you have used most often will show themselves in the landscape of your life.

## PIERCING WORDS

Still, despite the fact that they carry so much creation power, we are all guilty of wasting the majority of our words. Too often, we use them in a way that has little impact. We choose words that can be easily forgotten. But when you and I commit to living a tongue-pierced lifestyle, our words become reignited for a greater purpose. We suddenly become conscious of using them in a way that will change the course of our personal story, and perhaps even the course of history, for the better.

Consider some of the words that have stepped out of the deluge to become a lasting part of our social fabric:

"The only thing we have to fear is fear itself."
—Franklin Roosevelt

"Ask not what your country can do for you, but
what you can do for your country."

—John F. Kennedy

"Go ahead; make my day."

—Clint Eastwood in *Dirty Harry*

"I have a dream that my four little children will
one day live in a nation where they will not
be judged by the color of their skin but by the
content of their character."

—Dr. Martin Luther King Jr.

"I think this is the beginning of a beautiful
friendship."

—Humphrey Bogart in *Casablanca*

"Mr. Gorbachev, tear down this wall!"

—Ronald Reagan

Why have these words become ingrained in the context of our
national story, while the words of so many other speeches, films, and
the like have gone by the wayside? There must be something special
about these words that cling to our collective consciousness.

Similarly, I bet you can remember certain words that have risen
above the common clamor in your life and impacted you significantly.
Maybe a parent said something to you that you can still hear ringing in
your ear, or a teacher made a comment that has directed your course in
life. What caused those particular words to take root while others have
been so easily forgotten? One simple thing: they pierced your heart.

In these pages, we've examined how your words reflect the
condition of your heart, how they grow directly out of what's going

on inside you. Beyond that, the heart also determines which words stick with you and which ones slip right on by. Words that make a lasting impact are words that touch your heart, either positively or negatively. When you understand this reality, you've discovered the key to speaking words that stay with people, change lives, and impact the world around you. Simply choose words that will resonate with people at their core. Here are a few ways to do just that.

## USE YOUR WORDS TO BRING HOPE TO SOMEONE WHO IS STRUGGLING.

When President Roosevelt said, "The only thing we have to fear is fear itself," he was speaking to a country in the depths of the Great Depression. Many of his listeners didn't know whether or not their children would have enough to eat that day or if they were going to be able to hold their families together until things got better. President Roosevelt's confident, encouraging words struck a chord in the hearts of these desperate Americans. His reassuring message gave them hope that things were going to be okay, that brighter days were ahead. Roosevelt's words of hope gave his struggling listeners the resolve to fight another day. (To hear a full audio recording of President Roosevelt's 1933 inaugural address, go to TonguePierced.com.)

You and I probably aren't ever going to be speaking from a presidential platform, but there are struggling people around us every day who need the infusion of hope that our words can bring. There are people in our families, in our schools, in our workplaces, and in our churches clawing their way through difficult circumstances who desperately need to hear a word of encouragement. Our words of optimism spoken in love to the people in our world who are struggling have the potential for significant impact. They can give the recipient the shot of strength he needs to keep going.

Too often, our natural tendency is to speak the opposite of hope when people are struggling. Instead of encouraging them, we point out the mistakes they've made or how they could have done things differently to avoid the situation they're in. We think our words are teaching them to make better choices next time, but all we're really doing is hurting them even more. *Should haves* and *could haves* don't help anyone going through a hard time. If you want to use your words in a way that will have a positive and lasting impact rather than causing more harm, choose words of hope. Choose words that pierce the heart with light.

## USE YOUR WORDS TO CONFRONT INJUSTICE.

Dr. Martin Luther King's "I Have a Dream" speech is seared into our collective cultural consciousness not because of his eloquence or the poetry of his words but because of the courage it took to speak them. His 1963 address on the Washington Mall struck a nerve throughout the country and lives on today because it directly confronted the injustice rampant in our nation. Even now, Dr. King's words continue to give hope to those around the world facing oppression. (To read a full transcript of the "I Have a Dream" speech, go to TonguePierced.com.)

Ronald Reagan's words standing in front of the Berlin Wall in 1987 still resonate throughout history for the same reason. The words themselves—"Mr. Gorbachev, tear down this wall!"—weren't remarkable in their own right, but the backdrop of injustice he was standing against made them so. President Reagan was speaking for the millions of people on the other side of that wall yearning to be free from the oppression of a harsh dictatorship. His cry for freedom pierced the hearts of those who had been fighting injustice for so long, not to mention the hearts of observers around the world. (To see a video clip of this historic moment, go to TonguePierced.com.)

If you and I want to speak words that last—words that influence not only us directly but also the world around us—we can't sit idly by when we see an injustice being done. We have an obligation to help bring truth to the forefront. As Paul wrote,

> [Love] does not rejoice about injustice but rejoices
> whenever the truth wins out. (1 Cor. 13:6)

When God is in control of your heart, injustice won't sit well with you. You won't be able to remain silent when you see someone being taken advantage of or see a wrong that needs to be made right. Be sensitive to the injustices God brings to your attention so you can use your words to bring light to the dark situation.

## USE YOUR WORDS TO EXPRESS FAITH IN GOD.

If you've never trusted God with your life, take a minute to seriously consider the following question: *What do you have faith in?* Whom do you have faith in? Yourself? Your spouse? Your business partners? A religious tradition? The universe? An ephemeral God? On what kind of faith foundation are you building your life? Whether you realize it or not, you are building your life on faith in something. We all have a set of beliefs through which we filter the world. Over

time, those beliefs, whether positive or negative, build the foundation for our lives. But the only foundation worthy of building on
is the foundation of faith in God and his Son, Jesus Christ. In the
Gospels, Jesus himself said, "I am the way, the truth, and the life. No
one can come to the Father except through me" (John 14:6). Later,
he asked his own disciples—people who had walked with him for
years, seen him perform miracles, and listened to his teaching and his
claims—this: "Who do you say that I am?" (Mark 8:29).

Eventually, we all have to answer the same question; we all have
to make a decision about who we believe Jesus is. Either we embrace
Jesus as who he says he is, or we reject his teachings and continue on
our way.

It's intellectually dishonest to say you believe that Jesus was just
a great teacher or philosopher because, throughout Scripture, he
claimed to be divine. When it comes to his true identity, there are
only three options to choose from: (1) he was a lunatic for making
such claims; (2) he was the greatest con man who ever lived and is
still pulling the wool over people's eyes more than two thousand years
later; or (3) he is who he said he was. Take a look at how Cambridge
University professor and former agnostic C. S. Lewis positioned the
options:

> I am trying here to prevent anyone saying the really
> foolish thing that people often say about Him: "I'm
> ready to accept Jesus as a great moral teacher, but I
> don't accept His claim to be God." That is the one
> thing we must not say. A man who was merely a
> man and said the sort of things Jesus said would

not be a great moral teacher. He would either be a lunatic—on a level with the man who says he is a poached egg—or else he would be the Devil of Hell. You must make your choice. Either this man was, and is, the Son of God: or else a madman or something worse. You can shut Him up for a fool, you can spit at Him and kill Him as a demon; or you can fall at His feet and call Him Lord and God. But let us not come with any patronizing nonsense about His being a great moral teacher. He has not left that open to us. He did not intend to.[1]

When you and I acknowledge Jesus as the Son of God and accept the free gift of salvation that God has offered through him (see John 3:16), we gain forgiveness for our sins, a relationship with the one who created us, and eternity in heaven. All we have to do is use our words to confess the belief in our hearts. Look at what Paul wrote:

If you openly declare that Jesus is Lord and believe in your heart that God raised him from the dead, you will be saved. For it is by believing in your heart that you are made right with God, and it is by openly declaring your faith that you are saved. As the Scriptures tell us, "Anyone who trusts in him will never be disgraced." (Rom. 10:9–11)

When you believe that God sent Jesus to earth so you could be forgiven for your sins, find purpose and connection with God in this life, and spend eternity with him in heaven, you simply need to acknowledge that belief by speaking the most important words you'll ever speak in your life—the words that will usher in a transformation of your heart, the words that will alter the source of every other word you ever say and change the direction of your life for the better. If you have never spoken words of trust in God and Jesus, simply pray something like this:

*God, today, for the first time, I want to say I believe in you. I believe you loved me so much that you sent Jesus to die on the cross. I believe you raised him from the dead so my sins can be forgiven and so I can have a relationship with you. For the first time, I want to ask you to come into my life and transform me from the inside out.*

Just as God spoke the world into existence, you have the awesome privilege of speaking words that will connect you with him for eternity. He gave you that privilege, hoping you would choose to use it. If you just made the choice to place your faith in Jesus, welcome to the journey. (To learn more about your decision and to get some information on the steps you should take next, go to TonguePierced.com.)

## WORDS MATTER

Jesus stands as the ultimate example of how to use words that impact the world for good. He stunned crowds with the wisdom and depth of his teaching; he changed lives when talking to people one-on-one. His words still resonate with the heart of all humanity, not because of wordplay or eloquence, but because what he said constantly radiated

God's light and love. His words were filled with the power and conviction of his Father—and yours can be too.

One day you will be held accountable for the life you created and the influence you wielded with the words you chose to speak: "And I tell you this, you must give an account on judgment day for every idle word you speak. The words you say will either acquit you or condemn you" (Matt. 12:36–37). Every word that has ever left your tongue, and those yet to, will be judged for its merit. Every word of encouragement, praise, and love you've spoken will be revisited. Every negative, hurtful thing you've said to the people you love will come to light. You'll see the effects of every lie you've told and every judgment you've passed.

Between now and then, you have the opportunity to use your words in a way that brings life to the world around you; you have a chance to use your words to cooperate with God in creating your best future and reaching your full potential; you have the chance to use your words to show life-changing love to the people closest to you. Before Jesus was crucified, he said something interesting to his disciples: "Heaven and earth will disappear, but my words will never disappear" (Matt. 24:35).

Jesus said his words would last forever. As you commit to living a tongue-pierced lifestyle—to using your words to love God and love others—your words can last forever too. Not only can they change the way you walk through this world, but they can also influence the generations coming after you. You simply have to choose to harness them, to focus on using words that reflect the heart of Jesus himself radiating through you. When you do, your life will be better in the here and now and your legacy of love will live forever.

# NOTES

## CHAPTER 1—THE POWER OF WORDS

1. Maria Konnikova, "The Power of 'Once upon a Time': A Story to Tame the Wild Things," from the blog *Literally Psyched*, featured on *Scientific American*, May 8, 2012, http://blogs .scientificamerican.com/literally-psyched/2012/05/08/the-power -of-once-upon-a-time-a-story-to-tame-the-wild-things/.

2. Paul D. Tripp, "War of Words," *The Power of Words and the Wonder of God*, ed. John Piper and Justin Taylor (Wheaton, IL: Crossway, 2009), 24.

3. "Jailhouse Rot: The Death Penalty," *Investigate Magazine*, www .investigatemagazine.com/april00jail.htm.

## CHAPTER 2—WHAT YOUR WORDS SAY ABOUT YOU

1. Paul D. Tripp, "War of Words," *The Power of Words and the Wonder of God*, ed. John Piper and Justin Taylor (Wheaton, IL: Crossway, 2009), 37.

2. Geoff Waugh, "Twentieth Century Revivals," Revival Library, www.revival-library.org/catalogues/20thcentury/waugh.html.

## CHAPTER 3—THE MOST IMPORTANT CONVERSATIONS YOU'LL EVER HAVE

1. Nathan Bupp, "Follow-Up Study on Prayer Therapy May Help Refute False and Misleading Information About Earlier Clinical Trial," *Skeptic*, July 22, 2005, www.skeptic.com/eskeptic/05-09-02/.

2. Chuck Colson, "Can Prayer Heal?" BreakPoint, October 12, 2001, www.breakpoint.org/component/content/article/31/3215 -can-prayer-heal.

3. Colson, "Can Prayer Heal?"

4. Frank Newport, "More Than 9 in 10 Americans Continue to Believe in God," Gallup, June 3, 2011, www.gallup.com/poll /147887/americans-continue-believe-god.aspx.

5. Morgan Lee, "What Americans Pray For and Against (Per Max Lucado's LifeWay Survey)," *Christianity Today*, October 1, 2014, www .christianitytoday.com/gleanings/2014/october/what-americans -pray-for-against-max-lucado-lifeway-survey.html.

## CHAPTER 4—GO AHEAD—TALK TO YOURSELF

1. James Allen, *As a Man Thinketh* (West Valley City, UT: Waking Lion, 2007), 10.

2. Shad Helmstetter, *What to Say When You Talk to Yourself* (New York: Pocket Books, 1987), 62–71.

3. Allen, *As a Man Thinketh*, 13.

4. Stephen R. Covey, *The 7 Habits of Highly Effective People* (Provo, UT: Franklin Covey, 1998), 99–103.

5. Covey, *The 7 Habits*, 100.

6. Norman Vincent Peale, *The Power of Positive Thinking* (New York: Prentice-Hall, 1952), 46.

7. Helmstetter, *What to Say*, 85–87.

## CHAPTER 5—THE LANGUAGE OF LOVE

1. "63 Interesting Facts About … Marriage," Random Facts, http://facts.randomhistory.com/interesting-facts-about-marriage.html.

2. Paul Tournier, *To Understand Each Other* (Louisville, KY: John Knox Press, 1967), 13.

3. Paul Popenoe, *Marriage Is What You Make It* (New York: Macmillan, 1950), 4.

4. Robert Morris, *Power of Your Words: How God Can Bless Your Life through the Words You Speak* (Ventura: Regal, 2009), 29.

5. Catherine M. Wallace, "Seven Don'ts Every Parent Should Do," Catherine M. Wallace, www.catherinemwallace.com/Home/essays/seven-donts-every-parent-should-do.

6. John Trent and Gary Smalley, *The Blessing: Giving the Gift of Unconditional Love and Acceptance* (Nashville, TN: Thomas Nelson, 2011), 46, 47.

## CHAPTER 6—DEVELOPING AN ATTITUDE OF GRATITUDE

1. Will Bowen, *A Complaint Free World: How to Stop Complaining and Start Enjoying the Life You Always Wanted* (New York: Doubleday, 2007), 28–29.

## CHAPTER 7—THE ART OF CURSING

1. Jacquelyn Smith, "Dirty Words Can Cost You a Promotion," *Forbes*, July 25, 2012, www.forbes.com/sites/jacquelynsmith/2012/07/25/dirty-words-can-cost-you-a-promotion/.

## CHAPTER 9—WORDS THAT LAST

1. C. S. Lewis, *Mere Christianity* (London: The MacMillan Company, 1952), 40–41.

*We hope this book will be the beginning of an ongoing conversation. Please stay in touch with us at the website below.*

—Nelson Searcy and Jennifer Dykes Henson

Be sure to visit **TonguePierced.com** for your free online resources, including:

**Scripture References**—Access a complete list of verses in the Bible that deal with the power of words.

**Theological Studies**—Find in-depth examinations of issues addressed in the book, such as common grace and active versus passive curses.

**Historical Material**—Check out video clips and transcripts of some of the most influential words spoken throughout our nation's history.

*And much more ...*

 Nelson Searcy is the founding and lead pastor of The Journey Church, with locations in Manhattan, Brooklyn, Queens, San Francisco, and Boca Raton, where Nelson and his family reside. Previously, Nelson was director of the Purpose Driven Community at Saddleback Church. He is the author of ten bestselling books and founder of ChurchLeaderInsights.com.

 Jennifer Dykes Henson is a freelance writer based in New York City. Previously, Jennifer worked with Dr. Charles Stanley as the marketing communications manager for In Touch Ministries in Atlanta.